BESSER IN ENGLISCH

Grammatik

7./8. Schuljahr

von Brian McGredie
und Patricia East

Cornelsen
SCRIPTOR

Besser in Englisch, Grammatik – 7./8. Schuljahr –
wurde geplant und entwickelt von der Cornelsen & Oxford University Press GmbH, Berlin, im Auftrag des Cornelsen Verlag Scriptor, Berlin.

Verfasser David Clarke und Ingrid Preedy

Beratende Mitwirkung Helga Clarke

Gedruckt auf chlorfrei gebleichtem Papier
ohne Dioxinbelastung der Gewässer

Die Deutsche Bibliothek – CIP-Einheitsaufnahme

Clarke, Dave; Preedy, Ingrid:
Besser in Englisch / von David Clarke, Ingrid Preedy. – Berlin: Cornelsen Scriptor
(Lernhilfen von Cornelsen Scriptor)
Grammatik : für das 7./8. Schuljahr
ISBN 3-589-20881-3

11. 10. 9. 8. 7. Die letzten Ziffern bezeichnen
2000 99 98 97 96 Zahl und Jahr des Druckes.

Dieser Lernhilfe ist ein Lösungsheft zu den Übungen beigefügt.

Redaktion Christopher A. Caridia und James Abram

Illustrationen Caroline Eween, Hewett Street Studios, London und Christine Georg, Dortmund

Umschlaggestaltung Studio Lochmann, Frankfurt am Main

techn. Herstellung Svoboda, Prag

Printed in the Czech Republic

ISBN 3 – 589 – 20881 – 3
Bestellnummer 208813

Inhaltsverzeichnis

Möchtest du besser in Englisch werden?

Warst du in letzter Zeit mal krank und hast deswegen ein paar Englischstunden versäumt? Fühlst du dich bei Klassenarbeiten manchmal unsicher? Hast du vielleicht auch einiges schon wieder vergessen – oder von Anfang an gar nicht richtig verstanden? Ganz egal aus welchem Grund du Schwierigkeiten hast, dieses Buch wird dir helfen, dein Englisch zu verbessern!

Auf der nächsten Seite sind ein paar Tips wie du am besten mit *Besser in Englisch* arbeiten solltest:

♦ Das **Inhaltsverzeichnis** zeigt dir, was in den einzelnen Kapiteln angeboten wird. Du kannst das ganze Buch von vorne bis hinten durcharbeiten, oder die Themen heraussuchen, die du gerade nacharbeiten möchtest.

♦ Der **Computerbildschirm** am Anfang jedes Kapitels zeigt dir alle Themen, die in dem Kapitel vorkommen. Das hilft dir auch, genau das Richtige für dich herauszusuchen.

♦ Das **Wortfeld des Kapitels** bezieht sich immer auf ein Thema, das du wahrscheinlich in der Schule schon kennengelernt hast. Das Wortfeld soll dir helfen, Vokabeln zu wiederholen und zu üben.

♦ Die **Erklärungen** sind immer gleich aufgebaut. Die **Beispielsätze** zeigen dir, was in dem Abschnitt behandelt wird. Du solltest sie immer ganz gründlich durchlesen. Dann wird die Form vorgestellt und anschließend wird erklärt, wie man sie verwendet. Nimm dir immer genügend Zeit, damit du die Erklärungen auch richtig verstehst. Die Nummern im Kästchen beziehen sich auf die Beispielsätze.

♦ **Sally und 'Ping'** sollen dir bei besonderen Schwierigkeiten helfen!

♦ Die **Übungen** am Anfang jedes Kapitels sind einfach, werden aber zunehmend schwieriger!

♦ Der **Bleistift** sagt dir, daß es sich hier um eine Übung handelt, in der nur eine einzige Form eines grammatischen Themas vorkommt.

♦ Das **Auto** markiert eine schwierige Übung, in der alle Formen und Verwendungen des Themas gemischt und durcheinander abgefragt werden, genau wie bei Klassenarbeiten.
● Du kannst anhand dieser Übungen überprüfen, ob du alle vorangegangenen Übungen und Erklärungen richtig verstanden hast. Falls du die angegebene Endpunktzahl nicht erreichst, solltest du das Kapitel auf alle Fälle noch einmal durcharbeiten.
● Wenn du meinst, daß du ein Thema schon verstanden hast, kannst du diese Übungen auch sofort machen. So kannst du herausfinden, ob deine Einschätzung wirklich zutrifft. Falls du aber noch Fehler gemacht hast, solltest du unbedingt auch die Bleistiftübungen durcharbeiten.

♦ Die **puzzle pages** am Ende jedes Kapitels sind vor allem zur „Entspannung" gedacht. Auch hier werden Thema und Vokabeln des Kapitels noch einmal verarbeitet.

♦ Die **Lösungen** solltest du dir eigentlich erst ansehen, nachdem du die Übung selbständig durchgearbeitet hast. Wenn du aber Probleme hast, schau dir die Lösungen ruhig schon vorher an – es kann manchmal besser sein, so von „hinten nach vorn" zu arbeiten als einfach nur zu raten. Als „Mogelzettel" solltest du die Lösungen allerdings nicht benutzen – das hilft dir nicht.

Du solltest regelmäßig und gründlich mit dem Buch arbeiten. Das ist viel besser, als ein Kapitel übereilig und „in Panikstimmung" kurz vor einer Klassenarbeit durchzunehmen. Langsam Gelerntes sitzt sicher und fest!

Viel Spaß und Erfolg beim Arbeiten mit *Besser in Englisch*!

Die Autoren

1

A Das *simple present*

Erinnerst du dich?

	Hilfs-verb	Subjekt	Adverb	Verb	Objekt	andere Satzteile
1		I	always	**buy**	my clothes	at that shop.
2		The Bunns		**visit**	Scotland	every summer.
3		We		**don't watch**	TV	very often.
4	**Does**	Mr Scott	often	**work**		at home?
5		The Bunns		**live**		in London.

♦ Wir benutzen das *simple present*, um auszudrücken, was man immer, oft oder nie tut 1 – 4, oder um auszudrücken, daß ein Zustand unverändert anhält 5.

♦ Deshalb wird das *simple present* mit Signalwörtern wie *always, often, sometimes, never, usually, every day* usw. gebraucht, die einen wiederholten Vorgang bzw. eine immer noch geltende Situation beschreiben.

♦ Wenn es kein Hilfsverb im Satz gibt, benutzen wir *do/does*, um die Verneinung 3 und Fragen 4 zu bilden.

1 Schau dir die Tabelle an und dann beantworte die Fragen.

	The Bunns	Charley	Diana
Monday evening	go bowling (always)	play cards (usually)	clean her room (never)
Wednesday evening	work in the garden (sometimes)	watch TV (always)	practise guitar (always)
Friday evening	visit friends (usually)	read his comics (sometimes)	meet her friends (usually)
Saturday morning	do the shopping (never)	sleep until midday (sometimes)	help in a shop (always)
Sunday	have visitors (sometimes)	do his homework (never)	make breakfast (usually)

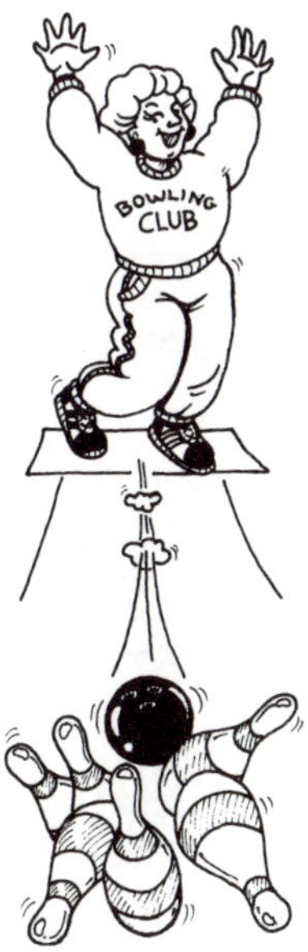

1 What do the Bunns do on Sundays?

The Bunns sometimes have visitors on Sundays.

2 When does Diana clean her room?

Diana ______________ her room on Monday evenings.

3 Do the Bunns go bowling on Saturdays?

No, they ______________ bowling on Monday evenings.

4 Does Diana always go to the cinema on Fridays?

No, she ______________ her friends on Fridays.

5 Does Charley play cards on Wednesday evening?

No, he ______________ TV on Wednesday evenings.

6 Do the Bunns always eat in a restaurant on Fridays?

No, they ______________ on Fridays.

7 When does Charley get up on Saturdays?

Charley ______________

on Saturdays.

8 What does Diana do when she gets up on Sundays?

She ______________.

2 Bilde Fragen, in dem du nach den unterstrichenen Satzteilen fragst.

1 Mr Bunn works at night.
When does Mr Bunn work?

2 Charley enjoys going for long walks in the woods.
What __________ doing?

3 On Monday evenings Diana goes to night school *(Abendschule)*.
__________ Diana __________ to night school?

4 Thousands of tourists go skiing in the Alps.
__________ thousands of tourists __________?

5 Colin can't play in the match because he has broken his leg.
__________ in the match?

6 Alison collects flower books. She's got nearly a hundred now.
__________ flower books __________?

7 Mr Hudd always goes to Wales in August.
__________ to Wales in August?

3 Sieh dir die Bilderpaare an, und sage, was die Personen gewöhnlich tun und nicht tun.

1 Alison doesn't play tennis.
She plays golf.

2 Pat and Betty __________
__________ by car.
They __________
__________ to school.

3 Most children ______________
______________ like eating fruit.
They ________________________
________________ eating sweets.

4 Mr Brown ________________
_________ always mend his car.
He _______________________
___________________his TV set.

5 Most girls ______________
_________________ like singing.
____
______________________________.

B **Das *simple past***

Erinnerst du dich?

1 – The girls' team **played** very well on Saturday.
– I know. I **watched** the match, too.

2 I **saw** a good film on TV last night. It **was** about life in China.

3 – **Did** you **go** to the youth club last week?
– No, I **didn't go** last week, but I'm going there tonight.

♦ Wir benutzen das *simple past*, um auszudrücken, daß ein Vorgang in der Vergangenheit stattgefunden hat und bereits völlig abgeschlossen ist. Oft wird dies mit Zeitangaben wie *yesterday, last week, in 1987, four years ago, once, when I was small* usw. verdeutlicht.

4 Hier ist Glorias Terminkalender für letzte Woche. Schreibe auf, was sie alles getan hat.

MONDAY 4 p.m., go to dentist	**FRIDAY** 6.30 p.m., practise for swimming match
TUESDAY buy birthday present for Uncle Bob	**SATURDAY** 10 a.m., meet Gilda at café
WEDNESDAY 5.15 p.m., have piano lesson	**SUNDAY** afternoon, prepare for English test
THURSDAY visit Aunt Mabel in hospital	

1 On Monday Gloria went to the dentist at four o'clock.

2 On Tuesday she ______________________ for Uncle Bob.

3 On Wednesday she ______________________ at a quarter past five.

4 She ______________________ in hospital on Thursday.

5 She ______________________ at 6.30 p.m. on Friday.

6 On Saturday Gloria ______________________ at the café at ten o'clock.

7 Gloria ______________________ on Sunday afternoon.

5 Nun sieh dir Glorias Terminkalender noch einmal an. Stelle Fragen mit *what?, when?* und *where?*, wie unten vorgegeben.

1 When did Gloria go to the dentist?

2 What ______________________ on Tuesday?

3 When ______________________ a piano lesson on Wednesday?

4 Where ______________________ Aunt Mabel on Thursday?

5 What ______________________ at 6.30 p.m. on Friday?

6 Where ______________________ Gilda on Saturday morning?

7 When ______________________ for her English test?

6 Benutze die unten angegebenen Verben, um diesen Text über Bobs Cousine Alison zu vervollständigen. Überlege dabei, ob du das *simple present* oder das *simple past* verwenden mußt.

✔ = richtig; ✗ = falsch.

be *(2x)* – buy – drive – get – go – have *(3x)* – not have – live *(4x)* – move – rent – say – tell – think – want – work

Now Alison ______________ [1] in London and ______________ [2] for a big bank. She ______________ [3] to London last year. Before that, she ______________ [4] in Glasgow. She ______________ [5] to school in Glasgow, and ______________ [6] her first job there, too.

Her parents still ______________ [7] in Scotland. Alison ______________ [8] a small flat in Glasgow, but now she ______________ [9] just one small room in a poor part of London. She ______________ [10] that life in London ______________ [11] much more expensive than it ______________ [12] in Glasgow.

But Alison ______________[13] a nice little car now. She ______________[14] it last month. She often ______________[15], 'Last year I ______________[16] a lovely flat, but I ______________[17] a car. This year, I ______________[18] a car, but I ______________[19] in one little room.' She ______________[20] her parents that next year she ______________[21] to have a nice flat and a nice car.

max. 21

Weniger als 16 Punkte? Wenn ja, arbeite bitte die Aufgaben 1 bis 5 nochmals durch!

7 In dieser gemischten Übung von Aussagesätzen, Fragen und verneinten Sätzen mußt du zwischen *simple present* und *simple past* unterscheiden. Setze die angegebenen Verben in die Sätze ein.

✔ = richtig; ✗ = falsch.

1 Miss Jolly ______________ (go) to the seaside every weekend during the summer.

2 – Mark only ______________ (learn) to swim last year and today he ______________ (be) the best swimmer in the school.
– I ______________ (not be) surprised. He ______________ (practise) every day. He ______________ (never do) anything else.

3 Bob often ______________ (help) at home. He ______________ (like) cooking. Last Christmas when his mum ______________ (be) in hospital he even ______________ (make) the Christmas dinner.

4 Mum, why ______________ (Tom/always/wear) my best T-shirts? Yesterday he ______________ (take) my red one and this morning he ______________ (have) my new blue one on. Why ______________ (you/not buy) him some?

max. 14

Weniger als 10 Punkte? Wenn ja, arbeite bitte die Aufgaben 1 bis 5 nochmals durch!

Ein Kreuzworträtsel

Um das Kreuzworträtsel zu lösen, mußt du bei jedem Satz ein sinnvolles Verb einsetzen. Achte dabei besonders auf die Zeitangaben.

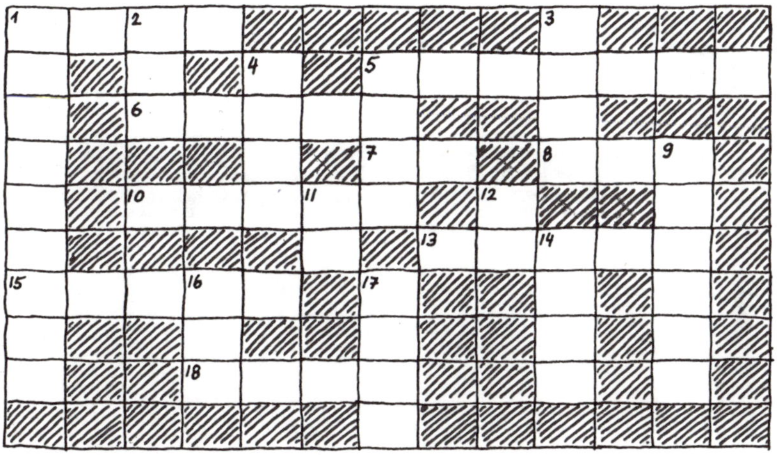

ACROSS

1 At weekends the children often ...... cards with their parents.
5 Have you all ...... your English books with you?
6 Yesterday my father ...... us to school because we missed the bus.
7 What's for tea? I ...... always very hungry after sport.
8 I ...... a very exciting film on TV last night.
10 I can't come and see you on Sunday. We always ...... my uncle then.
13 Mrs Clarke ...... us jokes at the end of the lesson.
15 My dad has to ...... in the afternoons because he works at night.
18 You've got a bad cold. Why don't you ...... some medicine?

DOWN

1 Brenda plays the piano well. She ...... for two hours every day.
2 If you ...... two and two, you get four.
3 Jim always ...... across the road instead of waiting for the green man.
4 Mrs Bunn ...... the shopping on her way home from work.
5 Our neighbours are horrible. They often ...... their poor little dog.
9 David ...... his car every Saturday.
11 Alison ...... a very good pianist.
12 Don't ...... late again, or you will have to stay after school.
14 John ...... school when he was 16.
16 Don't ...... too many toffees. They are bad for your teeth.
17 You can look round the shops by yourselves now, and we will all ...... at the bus in two hours. Don't be late.

2

Ⓐ Form und Gebrauch

Erinnerst du dich?

1 Alison **has decided** to stay on at school.
2 – Bronwen and Gareth from Wales **have** just **joined** our form.
– Oh. **Have** they **decided** what clubs they want to be in yet?
3 Joe **hasn't done** all his homework.

♦ Wir bilden das *present perfect* mit *have/has* + dem Partizip (der 3. Form) des Vollverbs.

♦ Bei regelmäßigen Verben wird das Partizip aus dem Infinitiv + *-ed* gebildet 1 2. Das Partizip (3. Form) der unregelmäßigen Verben mußt du einfach auswendig lernen 3.

♦ Um Fragen zu bilden, tauschen wir *have/has* und das Subjekt einfach aus 2.

♦ Wenn wir feststellen möchten, daß irgend etwas passiert ist oder, daß irgend jemand etwas getan hat – ohne aber zu erwähnen, **wann** dieser Vorgang sich ereignet hat – dann müssen wir das *present perfect* benutzen.

1 Der Lehrer muß die Klasse während der Stunde verlassen, um etwas zu holen. Nach ein paar Minuten herrscht ein fürchterliches Durcheinander, wie du im ersten Bild sehen kannst. Als der Lehrer zurückkommt, müssen die Schüler alles wieder aufräumen.
Sieh dir das untere Bild an, und benutze die angegebenen Verben, um aufzuschreiben, was die einzelnen Kinder getan haben.

~~clean~~ – empty – hang up – help – pick up – put – put away – wipe

1 Joe has cleaned the board and ____________ the chalk.

2 Betty ____________ the wastepaper basket.

3 Ben and Jim ____________ the books into the bookcase.

4 Alison ____________ the teacher's desk.

5 Joan and Susan ____________ the clothes.

6 Lillian ____________ the calendar on the wall.

7 Paul ____________ the teacher to tidy up the shelves.

B Das *present perfect* mit *for/since*

1 Joe and Alison **have known** each other **since** last June.
2 Jim **has lived** in Berlin **for** two years.
3 We **have been** here all afternoon.

♦ Wir benutzen das *present perfect* + *for/since*, wenn wir über eine Tätigkeit sprechen, die in der Vergangenheit anfing und bis zum Zeitpunkt des Sprechens noch andauert.

♦ Wir benutzen das *present perfect* + *for/since* vorwiegend mit den Verben *be, do, have, know, live* und *see*.
Im Deutschen benutzen wir dagegen das Präsens:

- Jim **has lived** in Berlin for two years.
  Jim **wohnt** seit zwei Jahren in Berlin.

2 Sind die folgenden Zeitangaben „Zeiträume“ oder „Zeitpunkte“? Schreibe je nachdem *for* bzw. *since* dazu.

1 ______ ten o'clock
2 ______ Christmas
3 ______ last summer
4 ______ ten minutes
5 ______ one month
6 ______ the last lesson
7 ______ a long time
8 ______ a week
9 ______ I last saw you
10 ______ the beginning of the term

3 Setze *for* bzw. *since* und die richtige Form des *present perfect* in die Sätze ein.

1 Joe has been (be) at this school for five years.
2 Where's Alison? I ______ (not see) her ______ this morning.
3 Mr Pryce ______ (know) his wife ______ they were both small children.
4 Ben ______ (not see) his uncle ______ several years.

5 I ______________________ (not be) very well ____________ Monday.

6 My brother ______________________ (have) his new motorbike ____________ two weeks.

7 They ______________________ (live) here ____________ they first came to Britain.

8 The poor animal is very hungry. He ______________________ (not have) anything to eat ____________ days.

4 Übersetze die Sätze ins Englische.

✔ = richtig; ✗ = falsch.

1 Sie ist seit heute morgen im Krankenhaus.

____

____

2 Joe wohnt seit fünf Jahren in Norwich.

____

____

3 Wir kennen uns seit Juni 1985.

____

____

4 – Wie lange bist du schon hier?

____

– Ich bin hier seit einer halben Stunde.

____

5 Ich habe diesen Füller *(fountain-pen)*, seit ich ein Kind war.

____

____

max. 6

Weniger als 4 Punkte? Wenn ja, arbeite bitte die Aufgaben 1 bis 3 nochmals durch!

Ⓒ Das *present perfect* und das *simple past*

1 – We **went** to London last weekend and **visited** all the famous sights. **Have** you **been** to London?
– Well, I'**ve been** to London several times, but I'**ve** never **seen the** sights.

2 – **Have** you **seen** Alison anywhere?
– Sure. I **saw** her in the playground a few minutes ago.

♦ Wenn ein Vorgang völlig abgeschlossen ist und wir nennen den Zeitpunkt, wann es passierte, dann müssen wir eine *past tense*-Form benutzen.

♦ Wenn wir den Zeitpunkt nicht nennen, dann müssen wir das *present perfect* benutzen.

5 Was haben sie alle bloß gemacht?
Die Klasse 4W war auf Klassenfahrt in den Bergen von Wales. Sie haben viel Spaß gehabt, aber leider gab es auch ein paar böse Überraschungen …

Sieh dir die Bilder auf Seite 18 an, und benutze die Verben unten, um zu sagen, warum die Personen jetzt zum Arzt gehen müssen. Benutze dabei das *present perfect* und das *simple past*.

be – ~~break~~ – burn – cut – ~~fall~~ – go – have *(2x)* – hurt – lose – trip *(stolpern)*

1 Mr Jones has broken his arm. He fell off a rope ladder.

2 Alison and Susan ______________________ themselves. They ____________ careless with the cooker.

3 Mrs Green ______________ her finger. She ____________ an accident in the kitchen.

4 Ben and Jim have got black eyes. They ____________ a fight.

5 Vanessa __________________ her feet. She ____________ walking in unsuitable *(ungeeignet)* shoes.

6 Colin ______________________ a tooth. He ____________ over a rock.

6 Setze die angegebenen Verben ein. Benutze das *simple past* bzw. das *present perfect*.

✔ = richtig; ✗ = falsch.

Last year we __________________ [1] (go) to the USA on holiday. We __________ [2] (fly) to New York. The airport __________ [3] (be) huge *(riesig)*. We ____________________ [4] (not walk) along the corridors. There ______________ [5] (be) moving walkways to take us from the plane to the customs.

'__________________________ [6] (you/be) to America before?' ______________ [7] (ask) the customs officer.

'Yes, we ________________ [8] (visit) California five years ago,' ______________ [9] (reply) my mother.

'How long ____________________ [10] (you/stay) then?'

'We ______________________ [11] (stay) just five weeks,'

______________ [12] (say) my father.

'______________________ [13] (you/bring) any fresh food, plants or animals with you this time?'

'No, we ______________________ [14] (not bring) anything like that,'

we ______________________ [15] (answer).

max. **15**

Weniger als 10 Punkte? Wenn ja, arbeite bitte Aufgabe 5 nochmals durch!

7 Übersetze die Sätze ins Englische.

✔ = richtig; ✗ = falsch.

1 Mr Jones arbeitet dort seit Anfang des Jahres.

____

____

2 Wie lange kennst du Alison?

____

3 1988 sind wir umgezogen.

____

4 Hast du „Starlight Express“ gesehen?

____

Wir haben es gestern abend gesehen.

____

5 Joe hat seine Hand verletzt.

____

6 Ich bin hier seit 3 Uhr.

____

Der Zug ist immer noch nicht gekommen.

____

max. **8**

Weniger als 6 Punkte? Wenn ja, arbeite bitte die Aufgaben 1 bis 6 nochmals durch!

Ein verrückter Stundenplan!

Leider hat der Schulcomputer wieder mal verrückt gespielt. Kannst du diesen Teil des Stundenplans der Klasse 4W trotzdem richtig zusammenstellen?
Trage die Lösungen in den leeren Studenplan ein.

MON	TUES	WEDS	THURS	FRI
MESSABLY				
OTRISHY	TRA	CUMIS	EGHPOYGAR	
STAHM	RENGAM	SYPHICS	LIGENSH	
REBAK				
TORPS	OLOBIYG			

MON	TUES	WEDS	THURS	FRI
ASSEMBLY				

3

Das *present perfect progressive*

A Form
B Gebrauch

Wortfeld: Aktivitäten

Ⓐ Form

1 You **have been watching** TV for nearly four hours. Don't you think that's long enough?

2 The children **have been making** an awful noise all day.

3 Peter **has been swimming** for over two hours now.

♦ Wir bilden das *present perfect progressive* mit *have/has been* + der *-ing*-Form des Vollverbs.

1 Setze die Verben in die Sätze ein.
Benutze durchweg das *present perfect progressive*.

1 Sally *has been doing* (do) the test for 45 minutes.

2 The sun __________ (shine) since early morning.

3 We __________ (lie) in the garden for three hours.

4 Freddy __________ (learn) his irregular verbs for ten minutes.

5 It __________ (rain) for four days now. What a holiday!

6 Alison and Jack __________ (play) tennis for two hours.

7 The British and the French __________ (talk) about a Channel tunnel since the 18th century.

8 Mrs Pryce __________ (try) to phone her friend in the USA for 30 minutes, but she can't get through.

B Gebrauch

[1] I **have been waiting** here **since 3 o'clock**, and the bus still hasn't come.
[2] Peter **has been looking** for his book **for over an hour** but he still can't find it.

♦ Wir verwenden das *present perfect progressive* für meist länger andauernde Handlungen und Vorgänge, die in der Vergangenheit begonnen haben und zum Zeitpunkt der Äußerung noch andauern.

♦ Im Deutschen benutzen wir in diesen Fällen häufig das Präsens mit dem Wort „schon", um auszudrücken, daß die Handlung bereits länger andauert:

- I have been waiting since 3, but …
  Ich warte **schon** seit 3 Uhr, aber …

2 Sieh dir die Bilder an. Schreibe auf, was die Personen tun, und seit wann bzw. wie lange sie die jeweilige Tätigkeit schon ausüben.

1 Dave has been writing that book since 12th May 1985.

2 Peter ______________________________ the marathon ______________ two hours now.

3 Sylvia and Dan ______________________________ midday.

4 Mark ______________________________ the washing-up ______________ over an hour.

5 John ______________________________ to music ______________ lunch.

6 Jack and Jill ______________________ in the dance marathon __________ more than 12 hours.

7 Meg ______________________ her motor-bike __________ 10 a.m.

8 We ______________________ the piano __________ half an hour.

3 Übersetze die Sätze ins Englische.

✔ = richtig; ✗ = falsch.

1 Ich stehe hier seit über einer Stunde.

____

____

2 Beeil dich! Du spielst mit deinem Essen seit fast einer Stunde.

____

____

3 Dominic, du trägst diese Jeans schon seit zwei Wochen.

____

____

4 Mr Brown baut sein Haus seit 1986.

____

____

5 Die Kinder machen seit Anfang der Stunde Lärm.

____

____

6 Joe und Anne räumen ihre Zimmer seit dem Frühstück auf.

____

____

max. 6

Weniger als 4 Punkte? Wenn ja, arbeite bitte die Aufgaben 1 bis 3 nochmals durch!

A lettersquare

Die *-ing*-Form der vierzehn angegebenen Verben sind in dem *Lettersquare* versteckt. 3 davon sind normal (►), 4 von oben nach unten (▼), 4 von unten nach oben (▲), und 3 schräg (◤ ◥) geschrieben. Kannst du die 14 *-ing*-Formen finden?

camp – do – drive – fish – garden – laugh – make – play – practise – read – run – swim – talk – wait

P	E	H	I	G	A	G	T	N	G	G	Z	O	T	F
V	A	L	E	N	N	I	L	T	N	H	E	B	A	Q
K	U	I	M	I	P	L	A	Y	I	N	G	R	L	Z
E	G	B	P	K	R	S	U	C	V	S	W	Y	K	P
F	M	M	X	A	A	S	G	D	I	R	C	O	I	Q
S	A	T	W	M	C	L	H	D	R	O	N	X	N	A
C	G	U	S	A	T	F	I	A	D	O	I	N	G	G
C	N	B	W	N	I	X	N	M	D	Y	O	Z	Y	P
A	I	K	I	C	S	T	G	B	J	X	J	M	N	G
W	N	U	M	D	I	L	I	E	H	W	K	Q	N	N
Z	E	K	M	R	N	E	V	N	H	G	S	I	A	I
U	D	E	I	T	G	S	K	P	G	O	H	P	I	N
F	R	V	N	J	V	Q	L	D	F	S	L	X	Q	N
G	A	J	G	U	R	E	A	D	I	N	G	V	B	U
W	G	Y	H	M	I	R	T	F	W	C	N	J	R	R

4

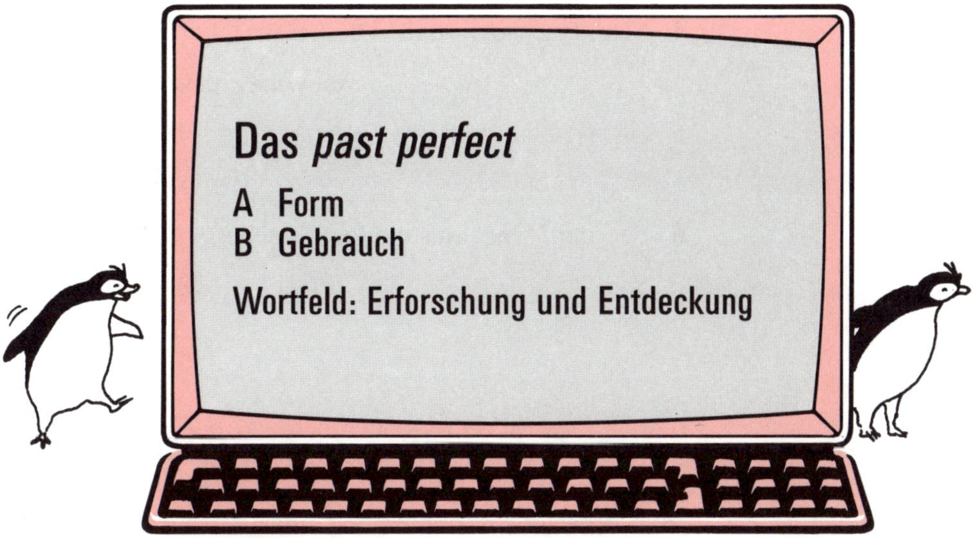

A Form

1 When old Mrs Cary died she **had lived** in the same house for over eighty years.
2 The thieves **had left** the bank by the time the police arrived.

◆ Wir bilden das *past perfect* immer mit *had* und dem Partizip (der 3. Form) des Vollverbs. Die Form ist für alle Personen gleich.

1 Letzten Monat besuchte Ben Taylor seine alte Schule. Er fand, daß sich inzwischen vieles geändert hatte. Setze die Verben ein. Benutze durchweg das *past perfect*.

1 Mr Havers was no longer there. He had left (leave) the school six years before.

2 When Ben was at the school, they ______________ (not build) the games room yet.

3 Miss Smith was now Mrs Jones, and Miss Brown, the Maths teacher, ______________ (become) Mrs Rossi. They ______________ (marry) other teachers several years before.

4 Ben's lovely old wooden desk wasn't there any more. The school

_____________ (buy) new plastic ones.

5 His old classroom was no longer grey.

It _____________ (be) painted green.

6 Ben didn't meet his old form teacher.

She _____________ (die) in 1976.

B Gebrauch

1 When Joe got home, the family **ate** supper.
2 When Joe got home, the family **had eaten** supper.

♦ Wir benutzen das *past perfect*, um zu verdeutlichen, daß eine bestimmte Handlung in der Vergangenheit bereits abgeschlossen war, als eine andere Handlung anfing:

1
▲ Joe kam nach Hause. ▲ Die gesamte Familie aß.

2
▲ Die übrige Familie aß. ▲ Joe kam nach Hause.

2 Lies dir zuerst die unvollständigen Sätze durch. Dann bilde sinnvolle Sätze, indem du die passenden Teile aus A – F und 1 – 6 kombinierst. Es gibt jeweils nur eine mögliche Lösung.

A When Christopher Columbus died he still didn't realize

B Some people say that Columbus didn't really discover America

C After sailmakers *(Segelmacher)* had made a new kind of sail,

D In spite of what Columbus had told his sailors,

E After Amerigo Vespucci had sailed south to Brazil,

F Columbus knew that there must be land to the west

1 people in Europe understood what Columbus had really done.

2 it was possible to sail against the wind.

3 that he had found a new world.

4 after he had seen pieces of bamboo on a beach in Portugal.

5 because Leif Ericson had landed in Canada in about 980.

6 after four weeks at sea there was still no land in sight.

A 3	B	C	D	E	F

3 Benutze das *simple past* bzw. das *past perfect*. Beachte bei jedem Satz die Reihenfolge der Handlungen.

✔ = richtig; ✗ = falsch.

1 When the ship *sank* (sink), they *had been* (be) at sea for a month.

2 After Lenny ________________ (see) a film about Captain Cook, he ________________ (decide) to read a book about him.

3 Anne ________________ (never ride) on an elephant before she ________________ (go) to London Zoo.

4 When Captain Scott ________________ (reach) the South Pole he ________________ (find) that the explorer Amundsen ________________ (already be) there.

5 When Mrs Cary finally ________________ (get) to the bus-stop, the bus ________________ (already leave).

6 When Mr Gilbert ________________ (look) at the signpost, he ________________ (realize) that he ________________ (take) the wrong road.

7 Mrs Green ________________ (arrive) at the post office at 12.30, but it ________________ (shut) half an hour earlier.

max. 14

Weniger als 10 Punkte? Wenn ja, arbeite bitte die Aufgaben 1 und 2 nochmals durch!

Das *past perfect* · Seite 30

Ein Quiz

Beantworte die folgenden Fragen zum Thema „Erforschung und Entdeckung". Die Buchstaben hinter den richtigen Antworten ergeben eine Lösung, die auch etwas mit dem Thema zu tun hat. Kannst du sagen was?

1 Who were the real discoverers of America?
Columbus (B) | the Indians (S) | Leif Ericson (E)

2 Where did Leif Ericson come from?
Spain (P) | Ireland (S) | Norway (A)

3 When did Ericson go to Canada?
about 1490 (K) | about 980 (N) | about 670 (O)

4 Who was the first man to reach Canada after Ericson?
Cabot (T) | Columbus (E) | Cook (D)

5 Who sailed down the Brazilian coast and discovered the Amazon?
Marco Polo (C) | Magellan (R) | Vespucci (A)

6 Where did James Cook discover many unknown islands?
the Pacific (M) | the Atlantic (W) | the Irish Sea (D)

7 What was the name of one of Cook's ships?
Mayflower (E) | Santa Maria (T) | Discovery (A)

8 What region did Captain Scott explore?
Scotland (T) | Newfoundland (M) | Antarctic (R)

9 Who was the first man to reach the South Pole?
Scott (A) | Amundsen (I) | Magellan (L)

10 In what year did an explorer reach the South Pole for the first time?
1908 (G) | 1896 (H) | 1911 (A)

The answer is ______________________________ .

This has got something to do with exploration and discovery because it was ______________________________ .

5

A Das *going to-future*

Erinnerst du dich?

1 When I leave school I'**m going to become** a teacher.
2 My boy-friend **is going to be** a mechanic.
3 We **are going to try and get** a job in London.

♦ Wenn wir über zukünftige Pläne und Vorhaben sprechen, die wir selbst bestimmen können, benutzen wir das *going to-future*.

going-to-future
am/is/are + going to + verb

1 Die Kinder sprechen über ihre Berufspläne.

Sieh dir die Bilder an und sage, was die Kinder beruflich machen möchten. Die unten aufgelisteten Verben werden dir dabei helfen.

build – catch – clean – cook – help – ~~look after~~ – repair – win

1 Sarah *is going to be a doctor*.

She *is going to look after* people when they are ill.

2 Charley and Tim ______________________ footballers.

They ______________________ a lot of games.

3 Betty ______________________ a car mechanic.
She ______________________ cars.

4 Adrian ______________________ a bricklayer.
He ______________________ houses.

5 Florrie ______________________.
She ______________________ a lot of criminals.

6 Michael ______________________.
He ______________________ wonderful meals.

7 Jenny ______________________ a window cleaner.
She ______________________ people's window.

8 Amanda ______________________.
She ______________________ Sarah look after ill people.

B Das *will-future*

Erinnerst du dich?

1 Mike **will be** 15 on 20th December next year.
2 Be careful with my CD player. You **will break** it.
3 There's the door bell. That **will be** the postman, I expect.

♦ Wir benutzen das *will-future*, um über zukünftige Vorgänge zu sprechen, die wir nicht selbst beeinflussen können 1.

♦ Wir benutzen das *will-future* auch, um eine Vorhersage zu machen 2 oder eine Vermutung zu äußern 3.

Gegenwart	Futur
must	will have to
can	will be able to will be allowed to

❷ Sieh dir die Wetterkarte genau an und sage, wie das Wetter in Großbritannien und Irland morgen wird.

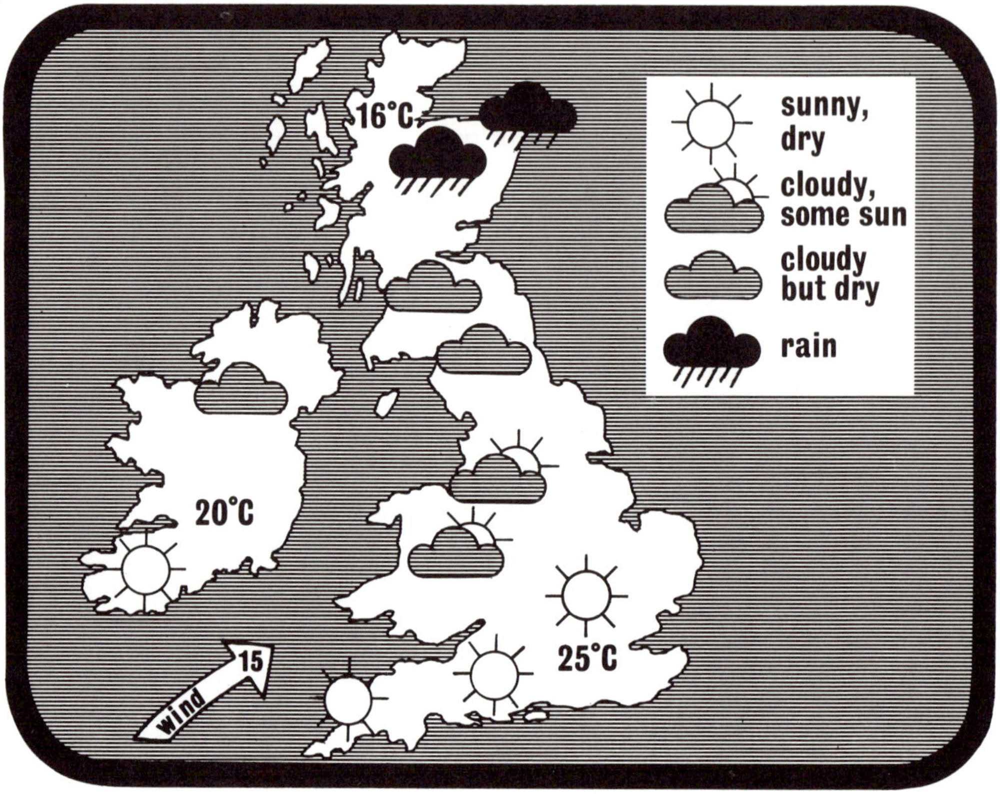

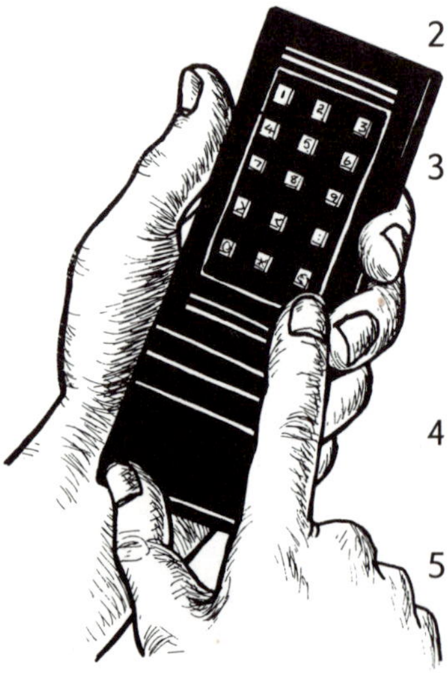

1 It *will be* (be) wet in the Highlands of Scotland.

2 In the London area you ________________ (see) the sun all day, and the temperature ________________ (go) up to 25°C.

3 The coolest place in Britain tomorrow ________________ (be) the Highlands. The temperature there ________________ (not go) above 16° C. You ________________ (not need) your swimming things.

4 In Wales and West England it ________________ (stay) dry, and you ________________ (even have) some sun.

5 In Southern Ireland the sun ________________ (shine) all day, and temperatures ________________ (climb) to 20° C.

6 The weather in Northern Ireland ____________ (be) the same as it is across the water in Northern England. You ____________ (see) a lot of cloud, but it ____________ (not rain) all day.

7 The wind ____________ (blow) from the South-West. We hope that it ____________ (bring) us some sunny weather.

3 Setze die angegebenen Verben ein. Benutze das *going to-future* oder das *will-future*. Denke daran, daß wir das *going to-future* nur für feste Pläne und Absichten benutzen; sonst verwenden wir *will*.

✔ = richtig; ✗ = falsch.

1 Bob is having an interview for a job as a bank clerk. I think he will get (get) the job. ✔

2 Colin is buying a ticket to Canada. He ____________ (fly) there to see his grandparents.

3 Jane has to do a test to get into university. If she's lucky, she ____________ (go) to Cambridge next year.

4 John is looking at the racing bikes in the shop window. He says that one day he ____________ (buy) a good bike.

5 Young Tim is too short to see the game properly. When he is older he ____________ (be) tall enough to see it.

6 Paula has bought a book on German. She ____________ (spend) her holidays in Germany this year.

7 Peter is very interested in politics. He hopes one day people ____________ (choose) him to go to Parliament.

8 Ted Brown has passed his driving test. Now he and Philip ____________ (start) a taxi service.

9 You ____________ (not get) a good job, Brian. You are so lazy.

max. 8

Weniger als 6 Punkte? Wenn ja, arbeite bitte die Aufgaben 1 und 2 nochmals durch!

Ⓒ Das *present progressive* mit zukünftiger Bedeutung

[1] – What **are** you **giving** Jim for his birthday **tomorrow**?
– I'm giving him a CD. And you?
[2] – What **are** you **doing** before you start your job **next August**?
– I **am working** as a waiter at the Al Café for a few weeks.

♦ Wenn wir über feste Pläne reden wollen, können wir statt dem *going to-future* auch das *present progressive* mit einem Adverb der zukünftigen Zeit, wie *tomorrow, next August* usw., benutzen.

4 Die Pengbornes sind immer sehr beschäftigt. Sie tragen ihre Termine in einen gemeinsamen Terminkalender ein. Sieh dir den Kalender an und sage, was die Pengbornes in den nächsten Tagen alles vorhaben. Benutze durchweg das *present progressive* mit einem Adverb der zukünftigen Zeit.

WEEK 21	
MONDAY	Julie, have ballet class, 5 p.m.
TUESDAY	Jim, practise guitar with Ben, 6.30 Mum, meet Joan for coffee, 3.30 Dad, play in darts match, 7.30
WEDNESDAY	Julie and Jim, attend youth club meeting, 6 Dad, take car to garage, 3 o'clock
THURSDAY	Hurrah! Today there is nothing to do!
FRIDAY	Julie, help Mum with shopping, after school Dad, pick up Bob Clarke for golf, 2.15

1 On Monday Julia *is having* a ballet class *at 5*.

2 On Tuesday Jim ____________________ the guitar with Ben ____________, Mrs Pengborne ______________________ Joan for coffee __________ and Mr Pengborne __________ ______________________ in a darts match ____________.

3 On Wednesday Julie and Jim __________________ a youth club meeting ______________ and Mr Pengborne ______________ the car to the garage __________.

4 The Pengbornes ________________ nothing on Thursday.

5 On Friday Julie ________________ Mrs Pengborne with the shopping ________________ and Mr Pengborne ________________ up Bob Clarke for golf __________.

Ⓓ Das *simple present* mit zukünftiger Bedeutung

1 I can't come tomorrow. I **go baby-sitting** on Thursdays.
2 My train **leaves** Berlin at 4 o'clock tomorrow.

♦ Genau wie im Deutschen wird das *simple present* gebraucht, um über **planmäßige Vorgänge** (Fahrpläne, Arbeitsstunden, Stundenpläne usw.) zu reden.

5 Peter und sein Freund Jack planen eine Rundreise durch Europa. Setze die angegebenen Verben in den Dialog ein. Benutze dabei durchweg das *simple present*.

Peter The train for Dover leaves [1] (leave) London Victoria every hour. We needn't worry. The ferry ______________ [2] (not go) until the train ______________ [3] (arrive).

Jack Fine. And how are we going to get to Cologne?

Peter No problem. Look, there ______________ [4] (be) a train from Ostend to Vienna. It ______________ [5] (stop) at Cologne. It ______________ [6] (go) an hour after the ferry ______________ [7] (get) in, so we'll have plenty of time.

Jack Yes, but that train is a bit expensive, isn't it?

Peter Well, we could go by coach *(Reisebus)*, I suppose. An express coach ______ [8] (leave) London for Cologne every day at 10 p.m. But it ______ [9] (take) much longer than the train. It ______ [10] (not reach) Cologne until midday the next day.

6 Vervollständige die Sätze mit einer passenden Form des Futurs. Nur eine richtige Lösung ist möglich.

✔ = richtig; ✗ = falsch.

✔ 1 – What are you going to do (do) when you leave school?

– Oh, I ______ (be) a vet, I hope.

2 – Hurry up, Betty. We ______ (miss) the train. It ______ (leave) at 10, you know.

– Don't worry. We ______ (must take) a taxi to the station then.

3 – I'm afraid I ______ (cannot come) to an interview next Friday. We ______ (go) on holiday the next day and I ______ (help) my mother with the packing.

– You ______ (never get) a good job like that!

4 Now you must be very careful with this microscope or it ______ (break). Then your parents ______ (get) a bill *(Rechnung)* from the school and they ______ (must pay) for it to be repaired.

5 The film ______ (start) at 8, so we ______ (meet) in front of the cinema at 7.45. And don't forget that you ______ (need) £2.50 to get in.

max. **14**

Weniger als 10 Punkte? Wenn ja, arbeite bitte die Aufgaben 4 und 5 nochmals durch!

Ein Säulenpuzzle

In den folgenden fünfzehn Sätzen werden Berufe beschrieben. Finde die jeweils richtige Bezeichnung und trage sie in das Puzzlegitter ein. In dem vollständigen Puzzle ergibt sich ein Lösungswort.

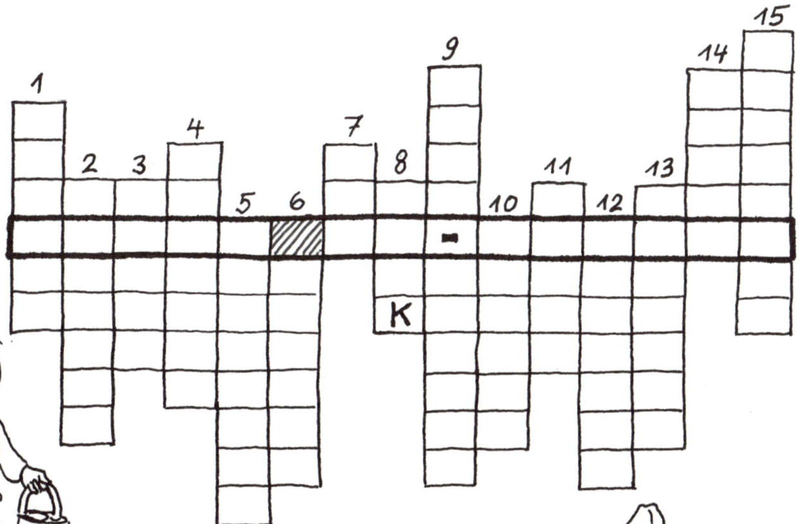

1 I like music and sing in concerts.
2 I carry a big bag and bring you your letters.
3 I wear a uniform and fly planes.
4 I help you when you have toothache.
5 I look after gardens.
6 People come and see me when they feel ill.
7 I am an 'animal doctor'.
8 I prepare food in a restaurant.
9 I take people around in my taxi.
10 I have got a farm where I grow things.
11 I help doctors look after people in hospital.
12 I teach in a school.
13 I make sausages and sell them in my shop.
14 I get up very early to make you fresh rolls.
15 I am a woman and I bring you your food in restaurants.

Das Lösungswort ist ______________________________.

6

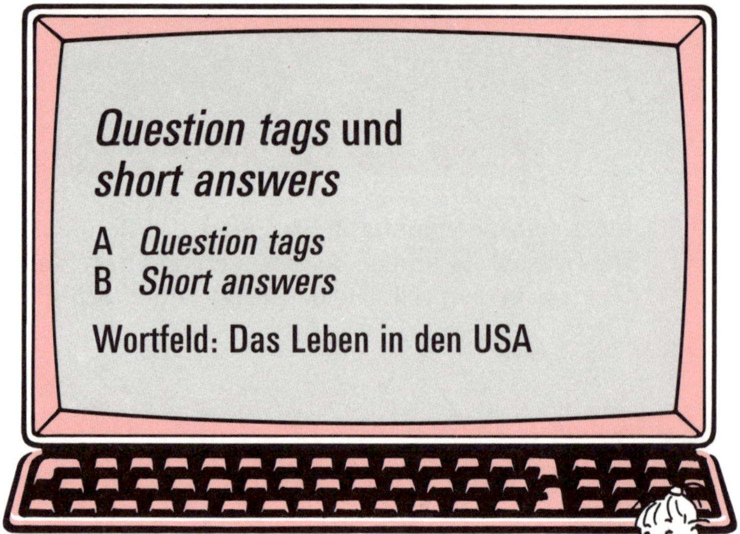

Question tags und *short answers*

A *Question tags*
B *Short answers*

Wortfeld: Das Leben in den USA

Ⓐ Question tags

[1]	San Francisco is in California, **isn't it?**
[2]	You can ski in the Rockies in summer, **can't you?**
[3]	Jefferson wasn't the first President, **was he?**
[4]	Alaska hasn't always belonged to the USA, **has it?**
[5]	The Americans drive on the right, **don't they?**
[6]	Christopher Columbus discovered America, **didn't he?**

♦ Die *question tags* wie *isn't it?, has it?* usw. am Ende der Sätze entsprechen den deutschen Frageanhängseln „nicht (wahr)?", „oder (nicht)?" usw.

♦ Wenn es ein Hilfsverb im Satz gibt, wird es auch verwendet, um das *question tag* zu bilden [1] – [4]. Falls aber kein Hilfsverb vorhanden ist, dann benutzen wir *do/does/did*, genau wie bei der Fragebildung [5] [6].

♦ Wenn das Verb im Hauptsatz bejaht [+] ist, dann ist das *question tag* verneint [–], und umgekehrt.

San Francisco	[+] is	in California,	[–] isn't it?
Jefferson	[–] wasn't	the first President,	[+] was he?

1 Hänge das *question tag* an die Sätze an. In allen Sätzen gibt es ein Hilfsverb, das du zur Bildung des *question tag* benutzen kannst.

1 Miss Sutherland has just moved from Scotland to America, hasn't she ?

2 Jack, you have been to the USA, ________________ ?

3 The Americans don't drive on the left, ________________ ?

4 July 4th is Independence Day, ________________ ?

5 Texas and California were once Spanish, ________________ ?

6 Susan, you shouldn't go on the New York subway *(U-Bahn)* alone at night, ________________ ?

7 We can go to a Baseball match on Saturday, ____________ ?

8 The Americans are very friendly people, ________________ ?

2 Hänge das *question tag* an die Sätze an. In diesen Sätzen gibt es kein Hilfsverb, das du benutzen kannst.

1 People speak English in the USA, don't they ?

2 The Pryces went to Florida last year, ________________ ?

3 You visited Hollywood, too, ________________ ?

4 Jack knows quite a lot about the USA, ________________ ?

5 I get a visa from the US Embassy *(Botschaft)*, ____________ __________ ?

6 The Navajo lived in Arizona, ________________ ?

7 We crossed the frontier between the USA and Canada at Emersen in Manitoba, ________________ ?

8 The shops stay open very late in America, ________________ ?

3 Übersetze die unterstrichenen Satzteile ins Englische.

✔ = richtig; ✗ = falsch.

1 Central Park ist in Manhattan, nicht wahr?

____

2 Amerikanische Kinder bekommen kaum Hausaufgaben, oder?

____

3 Die meisten Amerikaner können Englisch, oder nicht?

____

4 Lola kann nicht mit. Sie hat keine Zeit, oder?

____

5 Fast alle Amerikaner haben ein Auto, nicht wahr?

____

6 Viele Asiaten wohnen in Los Angeles, nicht wahr?

____

7 Neuengland war früher eine britische Kolonie, oder?

____

8 Zunächst halfen die Indianer den Siedlern, nicht wahr?

____

9 Los Angeles und San Francisco waren früher spanische Städte, nicht wahr? ______________________________

max. 9

Weniger als 7 Punkte? Wenn ja, arbeite bitte die Aufgaben 1 und 2 nochmals durch!

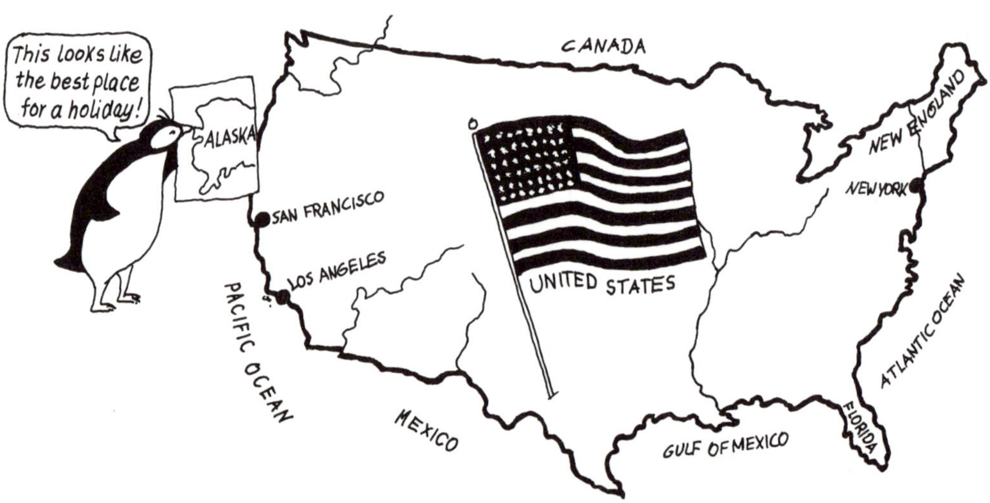

B *Short answers*

[1]	Lola **can speak** Italian.	[+] **So can Maria.** [−] **But Ben can't.**
[2]	They **must spend** less money.	[+] **So must we.** [−] **But Jack and Jill needn't.**
[3]	Hank **doesn't like** Chicago.	[+] **Neither does Jane.** [−] **But John does.**
[4]	I **like** hamburgers.	[+] **So do I.** [−] **But they don't.**

♦ Um Wiederholungen zu vermeiden, benutzen wir häufig *short answers*. Ausdrücke wie *so do I, neither does he* usw. entsprechen also dem deutschen „ich auch", „er auch nicht" usw.

♦ Genau wie bei *question tags* wird die Form der *short answers* auch durch den Hauptsatz bestimmt. Wenn es also ein Hilfsverb im Satz gibt, wird es auch in der *short answer* verwendet [1] – [3]. Wenn *aber* kein Hilfsverb im Satz vorhanden ist, dann benutzen wir *do* als Ersatz [4]

4 Schreibe zu den Sätzen eine geeignete Kurzantwort. Benutze die am Satzende angegebenen Namen. Achte dabei auf die Zeichen: bei [+] mußt du den angegebenen Satz bejahen; bei [−] mußt du den angegebenen Satz verneinen.

1 Gerda doesn't understand Spanish. (Maria)

[−] But Maria does.

2 Jane doesn't want to go to the pyjama party. (we)

[−] But ______________________________.

3 Marcia hasn't got an invitation to the barbecue. (I)

[−] ______________________________.

4 Harry forgot to bring some coke. (Wayne)

[−] ______________________________.

5 Susan didn't go to the hairdresser's. (Alison)

[+] ______________________________.

6 Jon went to a summer camp in Nevada last summer. (Hank)

[+] ______________________________.

7 I wasn't invited to the barbecue last year. (they)

[–] ______________________________.

8 They shouldn't smoke so much. (you)

[+] ______________________________.

9 Alison got a good grade at school last year. (Gerda)

[+] ______________________________.

10 Wayne can swim very fast indeed. (Jason)

[–] ______________________________.

5 Vervollständige die Sätze mit *so ..., neither ..., but ...*

✔ = richtig; ✗ = falsch.

1 Those boys are Sioux Indians and ______________ I.

2 New York isn't very clean and ______________ Detroit.

3 Lisa can't drive and ______________ Sharon.

4 Wayne doesn't know the way to the 'Caesar's Palace' ______ Grant ______________ .

5 Sharon never goes on the subway alone and ______ ______ Lisa.

6 Grant speaks Spanish and ______________ Jeff.

7 Sharon hasn't been at school for two days and ______ ______ Wayne.

8 Jeff only got into junior college because he's so good at baseball and ______________ Mike.

9 Grant likes dancing very much ______________ Wayne ______________.

max. 9

Weniger als 6 Punkte? Wenn ja, arbeite bitte diese Aufgabe nochmals durch!

6 Übersetze die unterstrichenen Kurzantworten ins Englische.

✔ = richtig; ✗ = falsch.

1 – Lisa liebt Spaghettieis. – <u>Aber ich nicht.</u>

____

2 – Grant wurde nicht in Houston geboren. – <u>Aber ich.</u>

____

3 – Wayne mag keine Hotdogs. – <u>Ich auch nicht.</u>

____

4 – Ich war letztes Jahr in Mexico. – <u>Martin aber nicht.</u>

____

5 – Ich konnte nicht schwimmen, als ich sechs Jahre alt war.

– <u>Wayne auch nicht.</u>

____

6 – Ich habe meinen Führerschein. – <u>Jason aber nicht.</u>

____

7 – Mein Vater arbeitet in Houston. – <u>Lisas Vater auch.</u>

____

8 – Grant wohnt in Dallas. – <u>Wayne aber nicht.</u>

____

max. **8**

Weniger als 5 Punkte? Wenn ja, arbeite bitte Aufgabe 4 nochmals durch!

Ein Säulenpuzzle

Beantworte die folgenden Fragen zum Thema *USA* und trage die Antworten in das Säulenpuzzle ein. Im stark umrandeten Feld ergibt sich ein Lösungswort.

1 What is the name of the US President's house?
2 A big US state which is not joined to any other state.
3 What is the name of the US flag?
4 What Texas city is famous for rockets and space research *(Raumforschung)*?
5 The real discoverers of America were the ......
6 In what city will you find the Statue of Liberty?
7 What was the first US President's first name?
8 The Apache, Sioux and Navajo are all Indian ......
9 How many cents are there in a US dollar?
10 What are the states in the north-eastern part of the USA called which were once British colonies?

The key word is ____________________ who was the ____________________________ of the USA.

It is also the name of a ______________ in the north-west, and of the federal ____________ in the District of Columbia.

7

A *May/may not, might*

may

1 – **May** I **get up** this afternoon, Mum?
(um Erlaubnis bitten = dürfen)

2 – No, Julie. The doctor said you **may not get up** until tomorrow.
(keine Erlaubnis geben = nicht dürfen)

3 Old Mrs Cary is very ill. I think she **may die**.
(Möglichkeit = „es könnte sein, daß ...")

4 You **may not smoke** in this part of the restaurant, madam.
(Verbot = nicht dürfen)

might

5 I **might see** you later. I'm not sure.
(vage Möglichkeit = „könnte")

6 Joe said Mrs Cary **might die**.
(Vergangenheit von may*, besonders in der indirekten Rede)*

1 Sieh dir die Bilder auf dieser Seite an, und setze *may, may not, might* in die entsprechenden Sätze auf Seite 49 ein.

1 – May we go (go) to that concert, Dad?

– No, ______________________ (go). Sorry.

2 Look at that cloud. It ______________________ (rain) soon.

3 – ______________________ (borrow) your new bike?

– Sorry. ______________________ (have) it today. I need it.

4 You ______________________ (go) in there. Look at the sign!

5 This sign says that ______________________ (smoke) on the bus, sir.

6 Oh, dear, the bus is going. That man ______________________ (not catch) it.

❷ Übersetze die unterstrichenen Satzteile ins Deutsche.

1 Don't visit Tim this week. You might catch his cold.

____

2 Simon may be late. He had to go to the doctor's.

____

3 You may get up today, but don't get dressed.

____

The doctor may want to look at you again.

____

4 – May I go to the youth club dance tomorrow?

____

– No, you may not. You still have a temperature *(Fieber haben)*.

____

5 – May Ann come round this afternoon, Mum

____

– No, I'm sorry, dear. You might be late for your piano lesson.

____

B Be able to, be allowed to

1 – **Will** Joe **be able to play** in the match next week?
– No. He **won't be allowed to do** any sport for several weeks.
2 I **wasn't allowed to get up** at all last week. I had flu.
3 I'm sorry I **wasn't able to come** to your party yesterday.

♦ Genau wie *must* können auch *can* und *may/may not* nicht alle Zeiten bilden. Die Tabelle zeigt dir, wie du die fehlenden Zeiten mit Ersatzhilfsverben bilden kannst.

Hilfsverb	Bedeutung	Vergangenheit	Futur
can	*Fähigkeit* *Erlaubnis*	was/were able to could	will be able to will be allowed to
may	*Erlaubnis*	was/were allowed to	will be allowed to

3 Lies dir zunächst die Dialoge und Sätze sorgfältig durch, und kreuze dann die richtige Lösung an.
Es gibt jeweils nur eine mögliche Antwort.

can/could, be able to, be allowed to

1 – Julia is allowed to speak ☐ can speak ☐ German.
– You're right. She'll be allowed to help ☐ 'll be able to help ☐ us when the German visitors are here.

2 My father says I couldn't go ☐ can't go ☐ on the trip unless I do better at school. If I don't, he won't give his permission and I won't be allowed to come ☐ am not able to come ☐

3 I was lucky yesterday. Mum phoned the hospital and they said I could come ☐ can come ☐ at once. They can see ☐ were able to see ☐ me because another patient couldn't come ☐ can't come ☐

may/might, be allowed to

4 – Mum, was I allowed to get up ☐ may I get up ☐ now?
– Not today, but Dr Pill said you might not watch ☐ will be allowed to watch ☐ television for a couple of hours tomorrow.

5 – Alison said she may come / might come out this evening, but she has got so much to do that she may not have / isn't allowed to have the time. And her dad said she will not be allowed to go / may not go out in the evenings for a week.

– Yes, but she wasn't allowed to go / may not go out in the evenings last week. She might leave / may leave the house now.

4 Übersetze die unterstrichenen Satzteile mit Hilfe eines geeigneten Hilfsverbs ins Englische.
Vergiß nicht, daß du manchmal ein Ersatzhilfsverb benutzen mußt.
✔ = richtig; ✗ = falsch.

1 Joe könnte heute abend kommen, aber ich glaube es nicht.

____

2 Darf ich die Rechnung *(bill)* bitte haben?

____

3 Wenn es warm genug ist, dürfen wir bestimmt schwimmen gehen.

____

4 Wenn du hart arbeitest, wirst du in einem Jahr viel Englisch verstehen können.

____

5 Ich wollte spielen, aber der Arzt sagte, daß ich noch nicht spielen darf.

____

6 Darf ich etwas zu essen haben?

____

Gestern konnte ich nichts essen, aber jetzt fühle ich mich besser.

____

max. 7

Weniger als 5 Punkte? Wenn ja, arbeite bitte die Aufgaben 1 bis 3 nochmals durch!

Puzzle Page

Schüttelwörter

Setze die Buchstaben in die richtige Reihenfolge, um herauszufinden, an was die Personen leiden.

1 Joe isn't at school today.
He has got a ______________ (DOLC).

2 Alison has got a ______________________________ (DHACHEAE).

3 Julie has eaten too much.
She has got a bad ______________________ (ASHTOCM HACE).

4 Wanda mustn't talk too much.
She has got a ______________________________ (ROSE TOHART).

5 Ben is in bed with ______________________ (ULF).

6 Susie can't write very easily.
She has a ____________________________________ (TUC NAHD).

7 Sally won't be able to dance for several weeks because of a
____ (NOBREK TOFO).

8 Jim must go to the dentist.
He has bad _________________________________ (HOTOTEACH).

8

Relativsätze *(relative clauses)*

A Relativsätze mit Relativpronomen
B Relativsätze ohne Relativpronomen
(contact clauses)

Wortfeld: Britische Regionen

A Relativsätze mit Relativpronomen

1 The man **who/that knocked Paul off his bike** is a doctor.

2 Half the men **that/who live in some parts of Liverpool** are without work.

3 These are the houses **which/that are for sale** at the moment.

4 That's the girl **whose parents come from Belfast.**

5 This is the house **whose roof was damaged in the storm.**

♦ Wir gebrauchen Relativsätze, um den Hauptsatz durch zusätzliche Informationen genauer zu bestimmen.

♦ Für **Personen** benutzen wir *who* oder *that* 1 2 und für **Sachen** benutzen wir *which* oder *that* 3.

♦ Um Besitz zu zeigen, benutzen wir *whose*, egal ob es sich um Personen, Sachen oder Tiere handelt 4 5.

1 Setze *who/that, which/that* oder *whose* ein.

1 Mrs Green is the woman who/that won the pools *(Lotto)*.

2 Nessie is a monster ______________ lives in Loch Ness.

3 The nice man ______________ works at the library is our neighbour.

4 The car ___________ radio was stolen belongs to my uncle.

5 That is the man ___________ wife was Miss Wales last year.

6 The bell ______________ is heard on the BBC is Big Ben.

7 We need a dog ______________ will guard the house.

8 The film ___________ won the Oscar was filmed in Ireland.

9 The bagpipes is a musical instrument ______________ is played in the Highlands of Scotland.

2 Der Programmierer hat schon wieder irgend etwas falsch gemacht. Er hat den Hauptsatz und den Relativsatz der Sätze durcheinandergebracht. Benutze die Buchstaben, um die Satzteile richtig zusammenzustellen.

1 Lord Nelson was a great admiral / which is visited by millions of tourists every year. (A)
2 London is a city / which is spoken in most parts of Wales. (B)
3 Ulster is a part of Britain / who came from Norfolk on the east coast of England. (C)
4 Welsh is a difficult language / which is full of beautiful lakes and forests. (D)
5 Kent is a farming area of South-East England / who came from Liverpool. (E)
6 The Beatles were a famous pop group / which has big problems at the moment. (F)
7 Scotland is the part of Britain / which is sometimes called the 'Garden of England'. (G)
8 The Lake District is a region of North-West England / which is famous for Scotch whisky. (H)

1 C 2 ____ 3 ____ 4 ____ 5 ____ 6 ____ 7 ____ 8 ____

3 Pete Brayne zeigt seinen Kindern alte Photos. Er gibt zu jedem Photo eine Erklärung. Verbinde die Sätze mit Hilfe eines Relativpronomens.

✔ = richtig; ✗ = falsch.

1 This is a little town in Cornwall. Its name is Portewe.

✔ This is a little town in Cornwall whose name is Portewe.

2 This is Uncle Benjamin. His family has lived in Norfolk for over 300 years.

This is Uncle Benjamin ______________________ in Norfolk for over 300 years.

3 These are some friends. Their home is in Ulster.

These are some friends ______________________ in Ulster.

4 This is a part of Scotland. It has beautiful mountains and lakes.

This is a part of Scotland ______________________ beautiful mountains and lakes.

5 This is York. The city gets a lot of visitors every year.

This is York ______________________ a lot of visitors every year.

6 This is Gareth Evans. His home is in Wales.

This is Gareth Evans ______________________ in Wales.

7 This is my school. Its buildings are very old.

This is my school ______________________ very old.

8 And this is my first girl-friend. Her name was Liz.

This is my first girl-friend ______________________ Liz.

max. 7

Weniger als 5 Punkte? Wenn ja, arbeite bitte die Aufgaben 1 und 2 nochmals durch!

B Relativsätze ohne Relativpronomen *(contact clauses)*

1 The hotel we stayed at is in an old castle.
2 The castle **that** has been changed into a hotel is in Scotland.

♦ Im Satz 1 benötigen wir kein Relativpronomen *that/which*, weil das Subjekt des Hauptsatzes *(hotel)* nicht gleichzeitig das Subjekt des Relativsatzes *(we)* ist. Wir benutzen also einen *contact clause*.

♦ Im Satz 2 dagegen ist das Subjekt des Hauptsatzes *(castle)* auch das Subjekt des Relativsatzes. Hier müssen wir also *that* oder *which* benutzen.

4 Entscheide dich, ob das Relativpronomen notwendig ist oder nicht. Wenn nicht, bilde einen *contact clause*, indem du das unnötige Relativpronomen durchstreichst.

1 Jim is happy with the new jeans ~~which~~ he bought yesterday.
2 Most of the children that she teaches enjoy her lessons.
3 The lady who won the money went on a world tour.
4 The dog who bit the postman belongs to our neighbour.
5 The steak that I had was awful.
6 Everything that people enjoy most seems to be bad for them.
7 The player who wins the match gets £1,000 and a cup *(Pokal)*.
8 Mrs Todd always gives us cake which she has made herself.
9 The postcard that we sent from Jersey still hasn't arrived.

5 In diesen Sätzen steht der Relativsatz am falschen Platz. Der Satz ist dadurch unsinnig.
Umkreise die Relativsätze und dann benutze einen Pfeil, um sie an die richtige Stelle im Satz zu stellen.

1 Mrs Cary has a parrot in a cage which can talk.

2 Joe saw an old man with a little boy who had white hair.

3 Children are free with their parents who are younger than five years.

4 Mrs Todd which is more than 150 years old has a cupboard for bread.

5 Mr Jones teaches the piano to my brother who is over 70 years old.

6 The piano is played by a pretty girl which has beautiful wooden legs.

6 Wo notwendig, setze ein Relativpronomen ein. Sonst laß die Sätze als *contact clauses* stehen.

✔ = richtig; ✗ = falsch.

✔ 1 Hollywood is a place *that* interests many people.

2 People ______________ live in Hollywood are not all film stars.

3 Many films ______________ were made here have become big hits.

4 A film ______________ many people enjoyed was 'E.T.'

5 An actor ______________ is now very popular is Clint Eastwood.

6 I saw the actress ______________ made this film yesterday.

7 What is the city ______________ the Beatles came from?

8 'Mull of Kintyre' is a song ______________ McCartney sings.

9 A TV series ______________ is very popular is 'Dallas'.

max. 8

Weniger als 6 Punkte? Wenn ja, arbeite bitte die Aufgaben 4 und 5 nochmals durch!

Ein Säulenpuzzle

Trage die richtigen Antworten aus dem Themenbereich „Regions of Britain" in das Säulenpuzzle ein. Wenn du alles richtig beantwortet hast, ergibt sich im stark umrandeten Feld eine Lösung.

1 The name of the city which is the capital of Wales.
2 The mountainous *(Berg-)* region of northern Scotland which is very popular among tourists.
3 A port on the east coast of Scotland which is the centre of the North Sea oil industry.
4 A big county in East Anglia whose first letter is 'N'.
5 The sea which separates the eastern side of Britain from the Continent.
6 The nationality of a person who was born in England.
7 Put 'er' on the end of 'London' and you get the name given to people whose home is in this city.
8 The nationality of people who come from the big island to the west of Britain.
9 A person who goes to sea in ships.
10 A Scottish word which means 'lake'.
11 Shakespeare was born in a town which is on this river.
12 The name of the city whose inhabitants *(Einwohner)* are called 'Geordies'.
13 The name of the port in South-East England which is the busiest ferry port in Europe.
14 The point of the compass which is opposite to north.

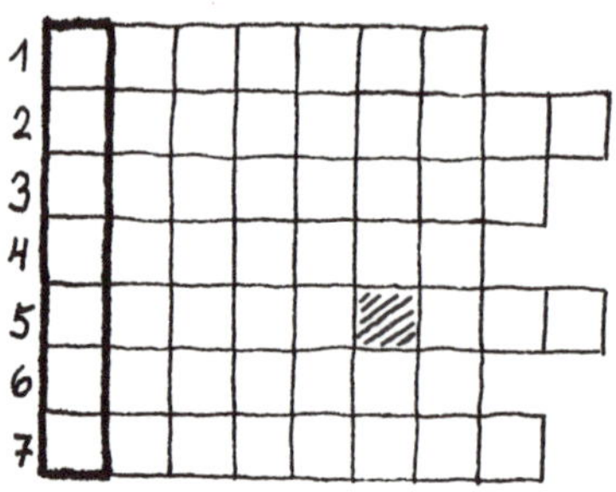

Die Lösung ist ______________________________.

9

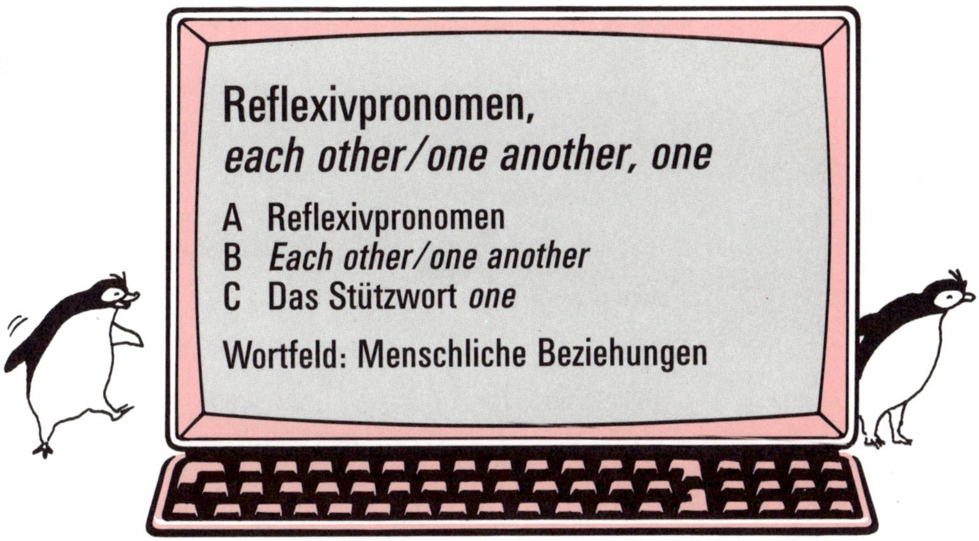

Reflexivpronomen, *each other/one another, one*

A Reflexivpronomen
B *Each other/one another*
C Das Stützwort *one*

Wortfeld: Menschliche Beziehungen

A Reflexivpronomen

1 Alison **cut herself** quite badly.
2 Jack's quite clever. He **made this table himself**.

♦ Hier ist eine Übersicht der Reflexivpronomen

I	**myself**
you	**yourself**
he	**himself**
she	**herself**
it	**itself**
we	**ourselves**
you	**yourselves**
they	**themselves**

♦ Wir benutzen Reflexivpronomen auch, wenn wir deutlich machen möchten, daß eine bestimmte Person irgend etwas selbst getan hat oder tun wird 2.

change	*sich ändern; sich umziehen*	open	*sich öffnen*
feel	*sich fühlen*	remember	*sich erinnern*
hide	*sich verstecken*	shave	*sich rasieren*
move	*sich bewegen*	wonder	*sich wundern*

1 Setze die richtigen Reflexivpronomen ein.

1 Jim hasn't got a teacher. He is teaching himself German.
2 Mrs Drew enjoys ______________ at the bingo every week.
3 The cake is on the table. Just help ______________ , boys.
4 Pat and Ann are old enough to look after ______________ when we are out.
5 I cut ______________ while I was getting the vegetables ready.
6 'DIY' stands for 'Do it ______________'.
7 Look at that poor bird. I think it's hurt ______________.
8 You sit down, Mrs Cary. We can get the tea ______________.
9 Bob didn't buy that cake. He made it ______________.
10 Alison, Jane, stop being so silly. Behave ______________.

2 Lies dir die Sätze durch und setze dann die englische Übersetzung der angegebenen deutschen Verben ein. Achte auch auf die Zeiten!

1 The door opened, and a girl came out. *(öffnete sich)*
2 I ______________ where my glasses are. *(wundere mich)*
3 Do you ______________ ? We met him last year. *(dich erinnern)*
4 They ______________ before they go to the concert. *(werden sich umziehen)*
5 I ______________ very well, Mum. *(fühle mich nicht)*
6 Al always ______________ in the evenings. *(rasiert sich)*
→ 7 Look at that parked car. It ______________. *(bewegt sich)*
8 What's wrong with Alison? She ______________ so much during the last few weeks. *(hat sich … geändert)*
9 The doors only ______________ from the inside. *(öffnen sich)*
10 The thief ______________ in the woods. *(versteckte sich)*

B *Each other/one another*

1 Pat and Ben always help **each other** with their homework.
2 Horst can speak good English. You will be able to understand **one another** without difficulty.

♦ *Each other* und *one another* haben dieselbe Bedeutung. Es ist egal, welches von beiden du verwendest. Sie haben die gleiche Form für alle Personen.

3 Sieh dir die Bilder an und benutze die Verben unten, um die Sätze zu vervollständigen.

love – ~~help~~ – hurt – know – shout at – play with

1 

Joe and Ben often help each other with their homework.

2 Mrs Cary and Mrs Todd ____________________ very well.

3 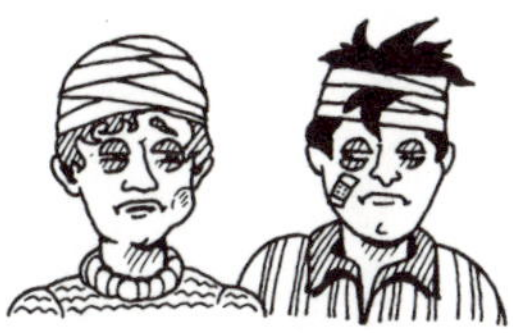

Jim and Bill ____________________ ____________ quite badly yesterday.

4 Mr and Mrs Payne ____________ ____________________ a lot.

5 

Please stop ____________________ ____________________ all the time.

6 Alison and Giles ____________ ____________________.

4 Setze *each other/one another* oder ein Reflexivpronomen ein.

✔ = richtig; ✗ = falsch.

1 The boy fell off his bike and cut ______________ badly.

2 In small villages everyone knows ______________.

3 Penfriends write letters to ______________, often to give ______________ practice in a foreign language.

4 Go and look at ______________ in the mirror. You've got egg on your face.

5 You shouldn't play with ______________ in church.

6 Ben, I'll do that. I'd like to do it ______________.

7 Twins often look like ______________, don't they?

8 Mrs Drew and her mother write to ______________ every week.

9 If you live alone, you start talking to ______________ when there is nobody there.

10 In self-service restaurants the customers fetch what they want to eat ______________. There are no waiters.

max. **11**

Weniger als 9 Punkte? Wenn ja, arbeite bitte die Aufgaben 1 bis 3 nochmals durch!

Ⓒ Das Stützwort *one*

1 That coat is too small. You need a **new one.**
2 – Which is your umbrella? – **The one** over there.

♦ Statt eines vorher genannten zählbaren Substantives benutzen wir nach Adjektiven das Stützwort *one/ones* 1. Im Deutschen gibt es kein Wort dafür. Wir lassen das Substantiv einfach weg.

♦ Auch nach *the, this/these, that/those* und *which* benutzen wir *one/ones* 2.

5 Sieh dir die Gegenstände an und sage dann, was du wählst. (Du wählst jeweils den markierten Gegenstand.)

1 – Which shirt do you want?
– *The one with long sleeves.*

2 – And the books?
– The ______________________.

3 – What about the apples?
– I would like ____________ for ________/1 lb.

4 – Which bike do you like best?
– ______________________.

5 – Which strawberries do you think are best?
– ______________________, of course.

6 – Which ball do you want?
– ______________________.

9 Reflexivpronomen, *each other/one another, one* · Seite 64

6 Übersetze die unterstrichenen Satzteile ins Englische.

✔ = richtig; ✗ = falsch.

1 – Welche Äpfel willst du?
– Ich will die roten.

____

2 Die blauen Socken sind kürzer als die gelben.

____

3 Diese Häuser sind teurer als die dort drüben.

____

4 Hast du einen neuen Comic? Ich habe alle die alten gelesen.

____

5 Diese Schuhe sind zu klein. Können Sie mir größere zeigen?

____

6 Welche Hosen nimmst du mit? Die blauen oder die braunen?

____

7 Hast du ein Buch mit? Ich habe keins.

____

8 Der Film war viel besser als der letzte Woche.

____

9 Ich finde diese Bluse zu teuer. Haben Sie eine billigere?

____

10 Welches Fahrrad hast du gemeint? Das silberne oder das gelbe?

____

max. 10

Weniger als 7 Punkte? Wenn ja, arbeite bitte Aufgabe 5 nochmals durch!

Beziehungen

Die unvollständigen Wörter auf der rechten Seite sind alle Personenbezeichnungen. Die jeweilige Person rechts steht in Beziehung zu der gegenüberstehenden Person auf der linken Seite.
Wenn du die Wörter richtig vervollständigst, ergeben die eingerahmten Buchstaben die Lösung.

1	mother	d a u g [h] t e r
2	teacher	___ [ ] ___ i l
3	shopkeeper	___ ___ ___ t o [ ] e r
4	doctor	___ [ ] ___ ___ e n t
5	house owner	[ ] ___ ___ g h b o u r
6	trainer	___ ___ ___ y e [ ]
7	pupil	___ [ ] ___ ___ h e r
8	parent	___ ___ i [ ] d
9	wife	___ ___ s b [ ] ___ d
10	detective	[ ] ___ i e ___
11	girl-friend	___ ___ ___ –f r [ ] ___ n d
12	guide	___ [ ] ___ ___ i s t
13	aunt	___ [ ] ___ l e
14	driver	___ ___ [ ] s e n g e r

Die Lösung ist ______________________________.

10

Die Wortstellung *(word order)*

A Sätze mit zwei Objekten
B Mehrfache Orts- und Zeitadverbien
C Adverbien der Häufigkeit und des Grades

Wortfeld: Englisch als eine Weltsprache

Ⓐ Sätze mit zwei Objekten

Hilfsverb	Subjekt	Verb	indirektes Objekt *(wem?)*	direktes Objekt *(wen?/was?)*	andere Satzteile
	Mr Todd	gave	**his wife**	**a kiss**	when he got home.
	Brian	sent	**Alison**	**some roses**	on her birthday.
Does	Paul	teach	**engineers**	**English**?	
Can	Julie	make	**me**	**a coffee,**	please?

♦ Sehr oft haben Verben wie *give, send, teach* usw. zwei Objekte, und zwar das **indirekte Objekt** (wem?) und das **direkte Objekt** (wen?/was?).

♦ Wenn es zwei Objekte im Satz gibt, dann steht das indirekte Objekt (wem?) unmittelbar vor dem direkten Objekt (wen?/was?).

1 Benutze Ziffern, um die Satzteile in die richtige Reihenfolge zu stellen.

1 (4) a letter (3) her penfriend in Japan (1) Kara (2) wrote

2 ◯ a photo of Witten? ◯ has ◯ her ◯ sent ◯ she

3 ◯ asked ◯ for some information about Japan ◯ her ◯ she

4 ◯ her ◯ taught ◯ three Japanese words ◯ Yuki Ito

5 ◯ so she ◯ three German words ◯ wrote ◯ Yuki Ito

6 ◯ a paper flower ◯ her ◯ made ◯ Yuki Ito

7 ◯ for Christmas ◯ Kara ◯ sent ◯ she ◯ the flower

8 ◯ did ◯ her ◯ is ◯ Kara ◯ reading? ◯ tell ◯ that ◯ her hobby

2 Bringe die Satzelemente in die richtige Reihenfolge und bilde vollständige Sätze. Achte auf die Wortstellung und die Zeiten!

1 teach/English/German technicians/Paul
Does Paul teach German technicians English on Mondays?

2 his mother/Joe/promise
________________ that he would be careful.

3 give/her little cat/Mrs Cary/some fresh fish
____
________________ yesterday.

4 a card/send/their friends/the Todds
____
________________ last Christmas?

5 lies/must not tell/people/you

____

__________, Joe.

6 her brother/Julie/make/some football socks

____

____________________ last week.

7 a letter/we/write you

____

__________ soon.

8 bikes/buy/Mr Pryce/the twins

______________________________ last year.

B Mehrfache Orts- und Zeitadverbien

	Zeit-angabe	Subjekt	Verb	Objekt	Orts-angabe	Zeit-angabe(n)
[1]		I	will see	you	**in town**	**tonight.**
[2]	**This July**	the girls	are going		**to France.**	
[3]		Peter	starts	work	**at Bunn's**	**at 9.30 on Monday.**

♦ Orts- und Zeitangaben stehen am Ende des Satzes [1] [3]. Soll die Zeitangabe besonders betont werden, kann sie an den Satzanfang gestellt werden [2].

♦ Gibt es mehr als eine Orts- bzw. Zeitangabe am Ende des Satzes, dann steht die genauere Angabe an erster Stelle [3].

♦ Die Reihenfolge ist immer Ort vor Zeit.

3 In den folgenden Sätzen sind einige Zeit- und Ortsangaben falsch eingesetzt.
Benutze Pfeile, um die falschen Sätze zu korrigieren. Alle Satzteile sind unbetont.

1 We had to speak English last summer in Denmark.

2 Luckily my brother can speak English. He is starting a new job in August in India.

3 Tom Jones sang his new hit last night on TV.

4 We are going to spend Christmas in Bristol this year at my parents' house.

5 There was an interview with the Chinese Prime Minister yesterday on the radio.

6 Ann's new flat is at the end of the road in the new house.

7 Let's meet at the pub tonight at about half past seven, OK?

8 Stefan will have to use in the Export Department *(Abteilung)* English next year.

4 Übersetze ins Englische.
✔ = richtig; ✗ = falsch.

1 Gestern sah ich Tom Jones im Fernsehen.

____

2 Die nächsten Olympischen Spiele sind 1992 in Barcelona.

____

____

3 Mein Vater lernt zu Hause am Wochenende Englisch.

____

____

4 Letzte Woche mußte ich nach Frankfurt.

____

____

5 Gestern sprachen wir beim Abendessen Englisch.

____

____

6 Während der Karnevalszeit *(carnival)* fahren wir zu Freunden in Norddeutschland.

____

____

max. 6

Weniger als 4 Punkte? Wenn ja, arbeite bitte die Aufgaben 1 bis 3 nochmals durch!

Ⓒ Adverbien der Häufigkeit und des Grades

	Subjekt	Hilfsverb	Adverb	Verb	Objekt	Adverb
1	Pat		**often**	visits	us.	
2	Ben	can	**usually**	play		**on Mondays.**
3	I		**hardly**	know	Jim.	
4	Rolf			has	English	**twice a week.**

♦ In unbetonten Sätzen stellen wir Häufigkeitsadverbien wie *often, usually, sometimes* und Adverbien des Grades wie *hardly, almost, nearly* usw. unmittelbar vor das Vollverb 1 2 3.

♦ Häufigkeitsadverbien wie *twice a week, every day, now and then* usw., die aus mehreren Wörtern bestehen, stellen wir genau wie Zeitangaben ans Satzende 4.

5 Benutze einen Pfeil, um das angegebene Adverb an die richtige Stelle zu setzen.

1 My brother works at the weekend. (sometimes)

2 Mr Todd gets home before 10 o'clock. (always)

3 The lesson has begun. (just)

4 Alison goes out with Brian. (still) (now and then)

5 Most American workers get two weeks holiday. (only)

6 Julie should be careful. She knows the man. (hardly)

7 Ben is late for evening class. (often)

8 We go to the cinema. (once a week)

6 Übersetze ins Englische.

1 Bernd kann kaum laufen.

Bernd ____.

2 Einmal im Monat besuchen wir meinen Opa.

We ____.

3 In England gibt es nur acht Feiertage *(public holidays)* im Jahr.

In England there ____

____.

4 Ab und zu sehe ich Max im Büro *(at the office)*.

I ____.

5 Manchmal finde ich Fußball ganz unterhaltsam *(entertaining)*.

I ____.

6 – Beeil dich! Du bist immer so langsam!

Hurry up! You ____.

– OK. Ich bin fast fertig.

OK. ____.

7 Bilde vollständige Sätze mit den angegebenen Satzelementen. Achte auf die Wortstellung und die Zeiten! In einigen Fällen mußt du außerdem Artikel und/oder Präpositionen ergänzen.

✔ = richtig; ✗ = falsch.

1 Mike/go/Australia/usually/winter

✔ Mike usually goes to Australia in winter.

2 Pat and Jenny/meet/always/park/Sunday afternoons

Pat and Jenny ______________________________

____.

3 I/listen/world news/hour ago/radio

I ______________________________

____.

4 We/can see/films in English/often/TV

We ______________________________

____.

5 Some New Yorkers/go out/alone at night/seldom

Some New Yorkers ______________________________

____.

6 You/must be/quiet/between 1 and 3/always/Germany/afternoon

You ______________________________

____.

7 Some parts/Holland/people/can watch/TV/four different countries/evening/sometimes

In some parts of Holland people ______________________________

____

____.

max. 6

Weniger als 4 Punkte? Wenn ja, arbeite bitte die Aufgaben 5 und 6 nochmals durch!

Ein Schütteldialog

Olaf aus Norwegen und Jutta aus Deutschland lernen sich während des Urlaubs kennen. Da keiner der beiden die Sprache des anderen spricht, müssen sie sich in Englisch unterhalten.
Der Dialog ist leider durcheinander gekommen. Benutze die Zahlen und Buchstaben, um die richtige Reihenfolge der Fragen und Antworten wiederherzustellen.

Olaf

1 Do you like living in a big city like Frankfurt?
2 Oh, so you live in a big city, then.
3 Hello, my name's Olaf.
4 Jutta? Oh, are you from Germany?
5 No, Bergen in Norway. And where are you from?
6 Yes, but there's lots to do and see there, isn't there?
7 I'm from Bergen.

Jutta

A Oh yes. There's plenty to do if you've got enough money.
B Frankfurt am Main.
C Yes, that's right. And you?
D I'm Jutta.
E Bergen? Are you from Holland?
F Not much. It's very noisy and crowded, I'm afraid.
G Yes, we do. In fact, we live right in the middle.

Die richtige Reihenfolge der Äußerungen lautet:

3 – D, ______________________________

____

11

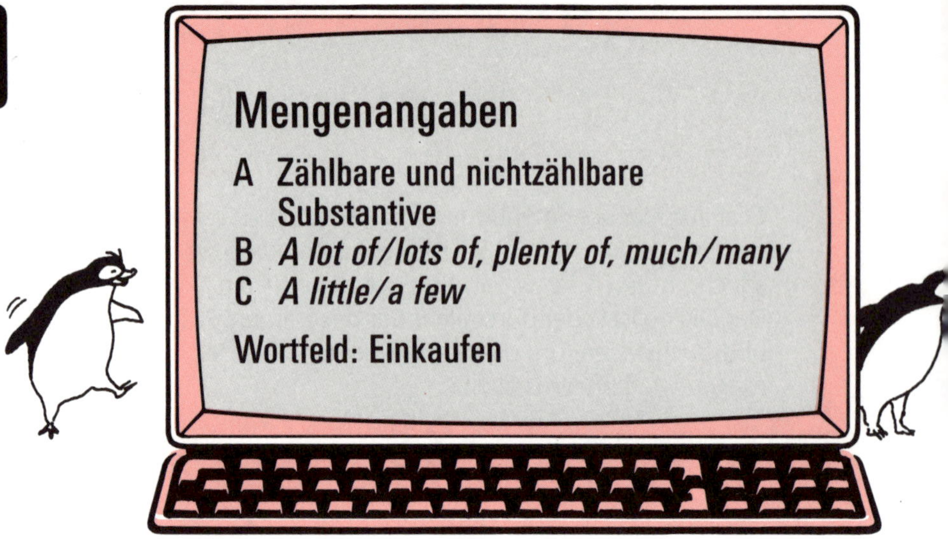

Ⓐ Zählbare und nichtzählbare Substantive

Erinnerst du dich?

1	I'd like **an ice-cream** and **a sandwich**, please.
2	Would you like **one** or **two eggs**, dear?
3	– Could you get **some milk**, please? – Sure, how much? – Oh, **three bottles** will be enough.
4	I must get **some trousers**. I've only got **two pairs of old jeans**.

♦ *Ice-creams, sandwiches* und *eggs* sind zählbar. Sie haben eine Pluralform und können dadurch mit *a/an* 1 und Zahlen benutzt werden 2. Wir sagen *an apple* oder *one apple, two apples* usw.

♦ *Milk, trousers* und *jeans* sind nichtzählbar. Sie haben keine Pluralform und dürfen deswegen nicht mit *a/an* oder Zahlen benutzt werden 3 4.

♦ Wir können nichtzählbare Sachen zählbar machen, indem wir ein geeignetes zählbares Nomen, z. B. *bottle of* 3 oder *pair of* 4, hinzufügen.

1 Zählbar oder nichtzählbar?
Sieh dir die Bilder an und ordne die Sachen der richtigen Spalte zu.

zählbar	nichtzählbar
biscuit,	chocolate,

2 Im folgenden findest du eine Liste von Mengenbegriffen, mit denen du die nichtzählbaren Sachen der ersten Übung zählbar machen kannst.
Ordne die Sachen den jeweils passenden Mengenangaben zu.

1 A piece of chocolate,
2 A bottle of beer,
3 A glass of beer,
4 A slice of

5 A pound of chocolate, ______________________

6 A spoonful of ______________________

7 A bowl of ______________________

8 A litre of beer, ______________________

9 A pair of ______________________

10 A bar of ______________________

B A lot of/lots of, plenty of, much/many

Erinnerst du dich?

1 – I've got **a lot of/lots of apples**. Do you need **any**?
– No thanks. I've got **plenty of apples** myself.

2 Mrs Todd hasn't got **many eggs** left. She'll have to buy **some**.

3 – Have you got **many CDs**?
– Not **many**. Only 5.

4 – We bought **a lot of lemonade** for the party.
– Yes, I know. We've got **plenty**.

5 Jim is very busy. He hasn't got **much time**.

6 – Is there **much milk** in the fridge?
– No, **not much**, and we haven't got **any** butter, either.

♦ Diese Mengenangaben werden wie folgt eingesetzt:

	bejahte Sätze	verneinte Sätze	Fragen
zählbar	a lot of/lots of plenty of 1	many 2	many 3
nichtzählbar	a lot of/lots of plenty of 4	much 5 6	much 5

3 Die Todds und die Braynes sind einkaufen gegangen.
Sieh dir die Bilder an und benutze *a lot of, much/many*, um die Sätze zu vervollständigen.

1 Mrs Todd has bought a lot of sugar, milk and cheese, but she hasn't bought ________ meat or ________ sweets and ________.

2 Mrs Brayne has got ________ wine, cakes and ________, but she hasn't got ________ milk, sugar or ________.

3 Alison has got ________ and ________, but she hasn't got ________ ________ or

4 Pete has bought ________ beer and ________, but not ________ or ________ mineral water.

4 Joe, Ben, Pat und Ann wollen eine Party geben. Zunächst stellen sie fest, was sie schon haben und was sie noch besorgen müssen. Vervollständige den Dialog mit den Mengenangaben unten. Es gibt nur eine richtige Lösung:

✔ = richtig; ✗ = falsch.

a lot of *(3x)* – any – how many *(2x)* – how much – many – much *(2x)* – not much – plenty – plenty of – some *(4x)*

Ann We've got quite ______________[1] lemonade.

Pat Yes, but ______________[2] coke have we got?

Ann ______________[3]. We've only got two bottles.

Joe OK, I'll get ______________[4] coke on my way home from school. ______________[5] bottles do we need?

Pat Twelve.

Ben Twelve? Good heavens, ______________[6] people are coming to the party? That's too ______________[7]. We've got ______________[8] lemonade already. We don't need so ______________[9] coke. Six bottles will be ______________[10].

Joe Ben's right. We haven't got ______________[11] money, either, and we still need ______________[12] food, don't we?

Ann Yes, of course. We've got ______________[13] nuts left from Christmas, but it would be nice to have ______________[14] cheese and ham as well.

Pat I'll ask my mum. I don't think we've got ______________[15] ham at home, but we've got ______________[16] cheese, so I'm sure she'll give us ______________[17].

max. 17

Weniger als 14 Punkte? Wenn ja, arbeite bitte die Aufgaben 1 bis 3 nochmals durch!

© *A little/a few*

1	I'm going to buy **a few apples** to eat on the journey.
2	There's only **a little milk** left in the fridge.

◆ *A few* (= ein paar) ► zählbare Sachen
A little (= ein bißchen) ► nichtzählbare Sachen

5 Vervollständige das Kochrezept mit *a little/a few*.

AN EASY OMELETTE

Ingredients (Zutaten)

______[1] eggs (three for an ordinary omelette, four if you are ______[2] hungrier), ______[3] spoonfuls of fresh milk, ______[4] butter, ______[5] salt and pepper (if you like).

What to do

★ Put the butter into a clean frying-pan, and heat for ______[6] minutes.
Break the eggs into a bowl and beat them ______[7] times with a whisk. Add the milk and beat the mixture ______[8] more. Add ______[9] pinches *(Prise)* of salt and ______[10] white pepper, if liked. Stir again.

★ Pour the mixture into the heated pan (not too hot!) and let it cook for one or two minutes. Turn the omelette over, and cook on other side for ______[11] seconds. (If you like, you can put ______[12] cheese or ______[13] small bits of ham into the omelette before you turn it over.)

★ Take the omelette carefully out of the pan and leave to cool for ______[14] time before you eat it.

6 Sieh dir die Bilder an und vervollständige die Sätze.
Benutze *a few, a little, a lot of, many* bzw. *much*.

✔ = richtig; ✗ = falsch.

1 There is only ______________________ in the glass.

2 Julia has got ______________________ in her basket.

3 The bus has not got ______________________ in it.

4 Mrs Drew hasn't got ______________________ left.

5 The milk bottle hasn't got ______________________ in it.

6 This teacher has got ______________________ to do.

7 There are not ______________________ to go before the new year.

8 There are only ______________________ toffees left.

max. **8**

Weniger als 6 Punkte? Wenn ja, arbeite bitte Aufgabe 5 nochmals durch!

Ein Versteckspiel

Sieh dir zunächst die Bilder an und überlege, wie die Sachen auf Englisch heißen.
Dann mußt du viele Buchstaben ersatzlos streichen, um neue Wörter zu bilden. Wenn du dies richtig machst, wirst du den Satz entschlüsseln können!

Der Satz heißt: ______________________________

____

12

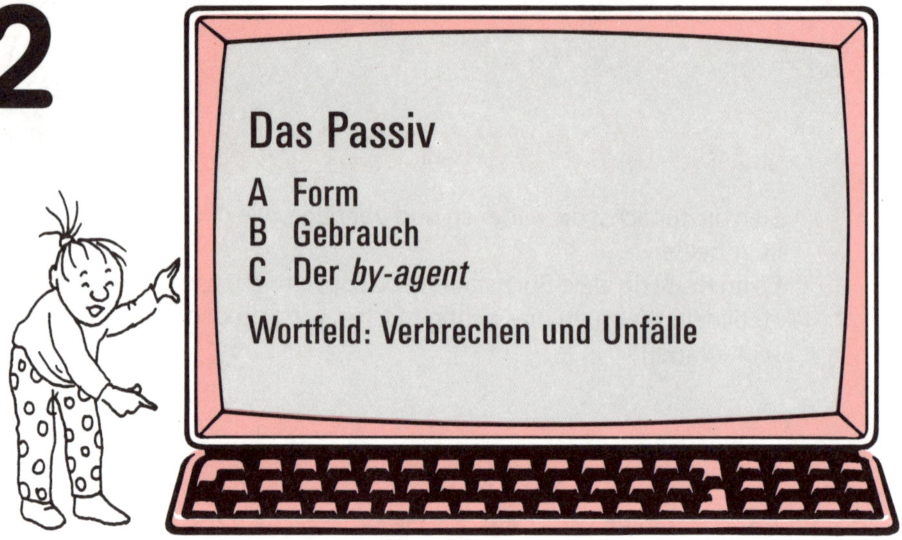

A Form

1 English **is spoken** in America.
2 A lot of money **was stolen** from that bank last night.
3 The kidnapped child **has just been rescued**.
4 The new hospital **will be opened** by Princess Diana.
5 A doctor **should be called** at once.

♦ *Is spoken, was stolen, has been rescued* und *will be opened* sind Passivformen.

♦ Wir bilden das Passiv mit einer Form von *be* und dem Partizip:

Zeit	*be*	Partizip
Simple present:	am/are/is	injured
Simple past:	was/were	stolen
Present perfect:	have/has been	rescued
Past perfect:	had been	broken
will-future: going to-future:	will be am/are/is going to be	opened sent

♦ Merke dir besonders, wie man Sätze mit Hilfsverben bildet:

Subjekt	Hilfsverb	*be*	Partizip	andere Satzteile
A doctor	should	be	called	at once.

❶ Lies dir den Bericht durch, und unterstreiche nur die Passivformen.

NORWICH, Weds. The Sheringham lifeboat was called out twice in heavy seas yesterday. At about 8 a.m. Bosun Davey West was telephoned by Cromer coast guards and asked to get a man off a German ship about two miles off the coast. The man had been badly injured and had to be taken to hospital in Norwich as quickly as possible. There he was operated on at once, and doctors were able to save the man's leg. Later, our reporter was told: 'The lifeboat crew is fantastic. The boat was launched in record time.' But the crew's work was still not done. The lifeboat had hardly been pulled back up the beach when it had to be launched again.

Some boys from London had been carried too far out to sea in a small boat and were soon in trouble. They were towed back to safety by the lifeboat. Said the father of one: 'I've never given the RNLI a penny, but now I know better. The crews of the lifeboats around our coast should be given all the help they need.'

❷ Vervollständige den folgenden Bericht, indem du *is/are* + Partizip (3. Form) einsetzt.

Do you know how a hit record is made[1] (make)? Well, first the song ______[2] (write) and a good group ______[3] (found). Sometimes the singers ______[4] (know), but quite often they ______[5] (not know). Then the song ______[6] (record) without the band. The words alone ______[7] (put) onto a tape. If the group isn't very good, the tape ______[8] (improve) by studio technicians. Later a professional band ______[9] (ask) to fill in the music. The music ______[10] (sometimes/play) by very good musicians from symphony orchestras. Then all the radio stations ______[11] (give) a copy of the new record. They ______[12] (often/pay) a lot of money to play it. If the record is a success, it ______[13] (sell) in all the record shops.

3 Setze die angegebenen Verben ein. Benutze dabei die Passivform des *simple past*.

Yesterday there was nearly a tragedy in Duke Street. Five-year-old Mandy Cooper was hit[1] (hit) by a car and ______________[2] (throw) into the path of a bus coming in the other direction. Luckily, Mandy ______________[3] (not run) over. She was small enough to go between the wheels of the bus. The car driver did not stop, but the car ______________[4] (soon/find) by the police. It ______________[5] (hid) in a garage in Rose Lane. The owner of the car ______________[6] (take) to the police station, but he ______________[7] (allow) to go home again. His car ______________[8] (steal) by someone early yesterday morning. Mandy ______________[9] (drive) to hospital in a police car. Doctors said last night that she was 'as well as ______________[10] (can expect)'. They added, however, that she ______________[11] (very badly/not injure).

4 Setze die angegebenen Verben ein. Benutze durchweg das Passiv. Beachte, daß alle Zeiten in dieser Übung vorkommen.

✔ = richtig; ✗ = falsch.

1 – Little Johnny Brown ______________ (not see) since last Tuesday. Do you think he ______________ ______________ (kidnap)?

– Don't be silly. He ______________ (collect) by his uncle and aunt. He has gone on holiday with them.

2 The supermarket ______________ (break) into last night, and over £5,000 ______________

__________ (steal). Hundreds of cars __________ __________ (stop), but the thief still __________ (not find).

3 Next week the winner of the competition __________ __________ (drive) to London in a Rolls-Royce and he – or she – __________ (welcome) to the best hotel in town by a famous TV star.

4 Soft drinks __________ (can buy) at that kiosk over there.

5 Radios __________ (should not play) on the beach.

6 – French and German __________ (teach) at British schools, but French __________ (learn) by more pupils than German.

– Yes, that's why only a few partners __________ __________ (can find) by German pupils.

max. 14

Weniger als 10 Punkte? Wenn ja, arbeite bitte die Aufgaben 1 bis 3 nochmals durch!

B Gebrauch

1 **Oil has been found** in Bavaria.
2 **Two fans were arrested** at the game.
3 **The hostages will be sent home** tomorrow.

♦ Wir benutzen das Passiv vor allem dann, wenn der Verursacher eines Vorganges entweder unbekannt oder nicht so wichtig ist. Das **Ergebnis** steht also im Vordergrund.

♦ Im Deutschen benutzen wir häufig „man", wenn im Englischen das Passiv verwendet wird.

5 Stelle diese Aktivsätze ins Passiv um.

1 Somebody stole Julie's purse at school today.
Julie's purse was stolen at school today.

2 One day doctors will find a cure for cancer.
One day ______________________________

3 Somebody has painted horrible pictures on the walls.
____
on the walls.

4 A man paid a million pounds for a Picasso last week.
____
for a Picasso last week.

5 They are going to build a motorway through the village.
____
through the village.

6 A businessman has already sold London Bridge to an American.
____
to an American.

7 Someone is going to teach Italian at our school.
____
at our school.

6 Simon Budd aus Norwich zeigt einer Gruppe aus Koblenz, der deutschen Partnerstadt von Norwich, seine Stadt.
Benutze die angegebenen Verben, um Simons Äußerungen zu vervollständigen. Achte auf die Zeitangaben!

✔ = richtig; ✗ = falsch.

1 This old church ______________ (build) in 1127, but it ______________ (not use) as a church any longer. It ______________ (just/buy) by the city and next year it ______________ (change) into a youth centre.

2 These lovely cottages ______________ (put up) in the middle ages. They ______________ (just/repair). Now they ______________ (live) in by old people.

3 We are now looking at the new ring road. It ______________ (finish) last May, but the plans ______________ (make) over 20 years ago. It ______________ (join) to the city centre car parks by tunnels.

max. 10

Weniger als 8 Punkte? Wenn ja, arbeite bitte die Aufgabe 5 nochmals durch!

C Der *by-agent*

1 That book wasn't written **by Enid Blyton**. It was written by Sarah Hill.
2 Pollution isn't caused **by animals**; it is caused **by people.**

♦ Wenn wir den Verursacher eines Vorganges in einem Passivsatz erwähnen wollen, benutzen wir einen *by-agent*.

7 Hier hat wieder jemand unsinnige Sätze geschrieben. Korrigiere die unterstrichenen Satzteile, um die Sätze sachlich richtig zu stellen.

1 Taxis are driven by bus-drivers.
Rubbish. Taxis are driven by taxi-drivers.

2 Trains are flown by engine drivers.
Nonsense. Trains ______________ by engine drivers.

3 Buses are cycled by seamen.
That's silly. Buses ______________.

4 Ships are steered by cyclists.
No. Ships are steered ______________.

5 Lorries are sailed by airline pilots.
That's wrong. Lorries ______________.

8 Schreibe die Sätze ins Passiv um.
Benutze einen *by-agent* nur, wenn es wirklich notwendig oder von Interesse ist.

✔ = richtig; ✗ = falsch.

1 Someone has stolen Ben's bike.

____

2 Carl Benz invented the motor car.

____

____

3 Did Columbus or Ericson discover America?

____

____

4 They built this church in 1556.

____

5 German scientists made the first rocket.

____

____

6 Has someone taken your coat by mistake?

____

____

7 You can buy stamps at that kiosk.

____

8 Somebody left the TV on last night.

____

9 Do people often borrow this book from the library?

____

____

10 They'll repair the car on Friday.

____

max. 10

Weniger als 8 Punkte? Wenn ja, arbeite bitte die Aufgaben 1 bis 7 nochmals durch!

Die Geheimnachricht

Der Detektiv findet die folgende Geheimnachricht in Freddy Fingers Hosentasche.
Sobald der Detektiv festgestellt hat, daß die Buchstaben „Z“ und „V“ in der Nachricht eigentlich „A“ und „E“ heißen, hat er sehr schnell herausgefunden, wo Freddy die Beute versteckt hat.

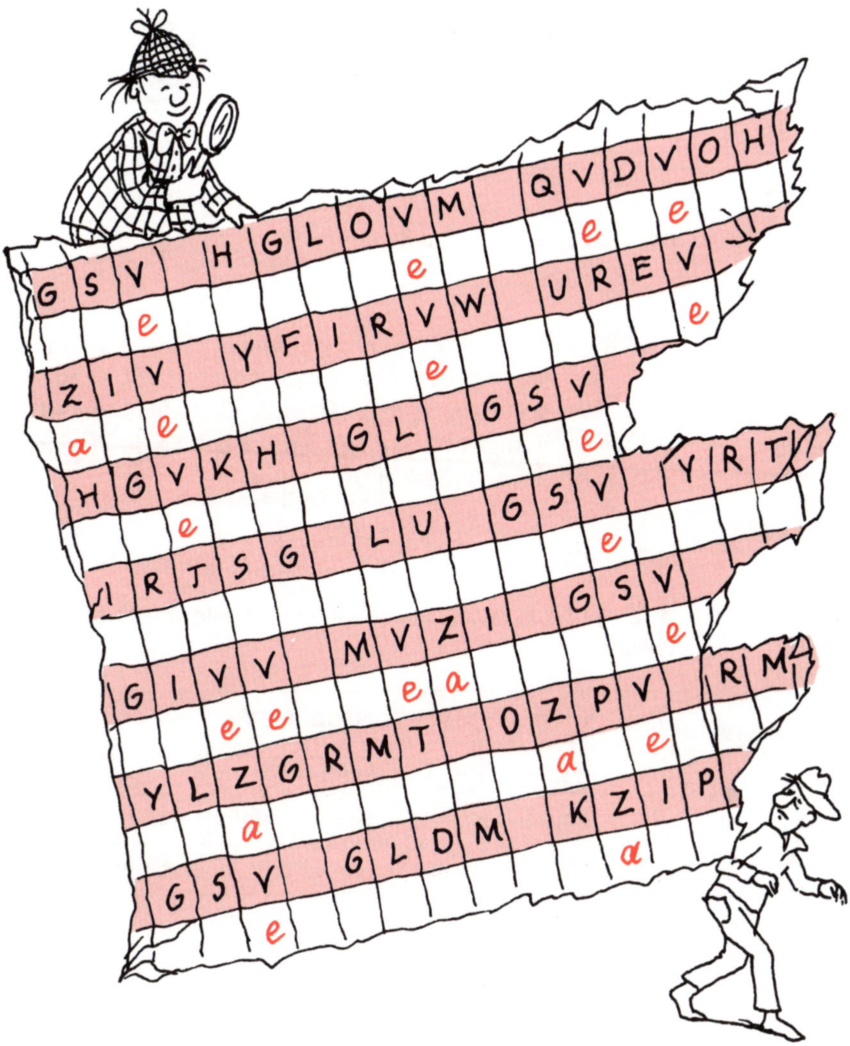

13

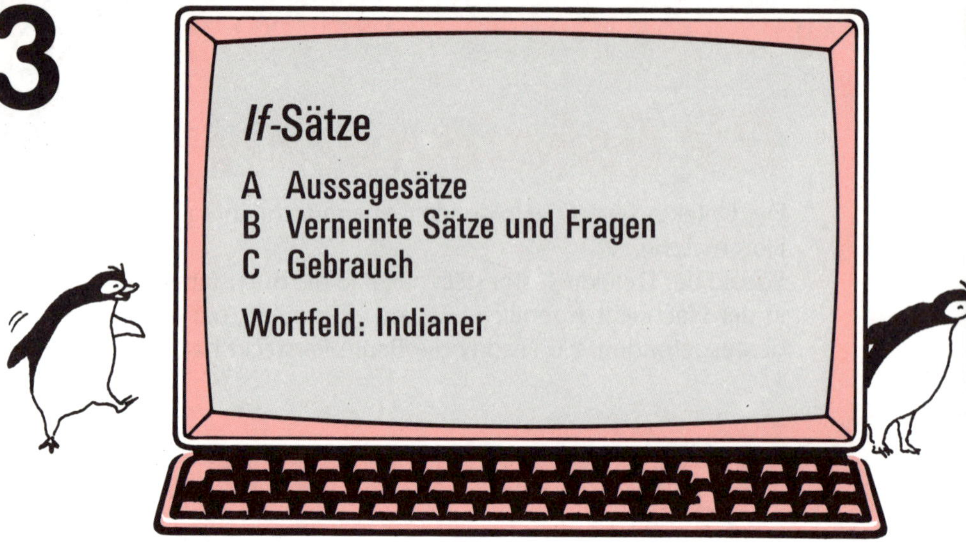

Ⓐ Aussagesätze

[1] If you **read** 'Winnetou', you **will find out** a lot about Indians.
[2] You **will find out** a lot about Indians if you **read** 'Winnetou'.
[3] If the settlers **were** more friendly, the Indians **would help** them.
[4] If the Indians **had not given** the settlers food, many of them **would have died** in the winter.

♦ Ein *if*-Satz hat zwei Teile, den *if*-Teil und den Hauptteil.

♦ Es gibt drei Arten von *if*-Sätzen, die alle verschiedene Zeiten aufweisen:

Typ	*if*-Teil	Hauptteil
1	simple present	will-future [1] [2]
2	simple past	would + infinitive *(Grundform)* [3]
3	past perfect	would have + participle *(3. Form)* [4]

♦ Es spielt keine Rolle, in welche Reihenfolge du die beiden Teile eines *if*-Satzes stellst [1] [2].

♦ Wenn der *if*-Teil an erster Stelle steht, dann trennen wir die beiden Teile mit einem Komma (,) [1] [3] [4].

1 Schreibe in die Kästchen am Ende des Satzes, um welche Art *if*-Satz es sich handelt.

1 If you are not there, we'll wait outside the café. [1]
2 We would go on holiday if we had enough money. [ ]
3 We'll see you at Ann's party if we go. [ ]
4 If you had practised more, you would have done better. [ ]
5 If Mr Bunn was friendly, he would get more customers. [ ]
6 The Indians wouldn't have attacked the settlers if the settlers hadn't stolen their land. [ ]
7 Columbus said, 'If we sail to the West, we will find land.' [ ]
8 If I'm there first, I'll get a table near the band. [ ]

2 Vervollständige die *if*-Sätze.

Typ 1

1 If the weather is good, we will go camping at the weekend. (be/go camping)
2 If I ______________ a holiday job, I ______________ ______________ some money. (get/earn)
3 The Indians said, 'We ______________ nothing to eat if you ______________ all the buffaloes.' (have/kill)

Typ 2

4 If the taxi-driver ______________ faster, we ______________ ______________ at the station on time. (drive/arrive)
5 A lot of pupils ______________ better at school if they ______________ to the teacher. (do/listen)
6 If the settlers ______________ to understand the Indians, they ______________ together peacefully. (try/live)

Typ 3

7 I'm sure that Mr Bunn ______________________ Brian a job if he ______________ more polite to him. (give/be)

8 If the white settlers ______________ their promises, the Indians ____________________ them alone. (keep/leave)

9 We ____________________________ the match if we ____________________________ harder. (win/practise)

3 Wähle ein sinnvolles Verb aus der Liste, und setze es in die entsprechende Lücke ein. Achte darauf, welchen *if*-Satz-Typ du benutzen mußt.

✔ = richtig; ✗ = falsch.

be – give – ~~hurry~~ – look at – move – teach – watch – win

✔ 1 If we *hurry*, we will catch the train all right.

2 The settlers said, 'If we have no food, perhaps the Indians ______________________ us some.'

3 The Indians ______________________ the fight if they had had guns and horses.

4 Tom Barton said, 'The Indians ______________________ us how to hunt if we gave them some guns.'

5 If you ______________________ the map on page 23, you would see in what parts of America the tribes lived.

6 He will get the wrong idea about the American Indians if he ______________________ those silly westerns.

7 The US government would have kept its promises if the Indians' lands ______________________ valueless *(wertlos)*.

8 Chief Joseph said, 'If the US cavalry attacks the village, we ______________________ north to Canada.'

max. 7

Weniger als 5 Punkte? Wenn ja, arbeite bitte die Aufgaben 1 und 2 nochmals durch!

B Verneinte Sätze und Fragen

1 If you eat less potatoes, you **won't be** so fat.
2 If you **weren't** so lazy, you would get better marks.
3 **Would you buy** that CD if you had enough pocket-money?

♦ Wir können – je nach Sinn – sowohl den *if*-Teil als auch den Hauptteil des Satzes verneinen 1 2.

♦ Bei Fragen dagegen wird nur der **Hauptteil** als Frage gebildet. Der *if*-Teil bleibt dabei unverändert 3.

4 Verbinde die links aufgelisteten Satzteile mit den Teilen rechts, um sinnvolle *if*-Sätze zu bilden.

1	If you had done your homework,	___	thousands of Indians would not have died of hunger.
2	If you don't prepare for the test properly,	___	the tribes would live at peace with the settlers.
3	Would you lend me your new CD	___	if you had had some food at home?
4	If the settlers didn't destroy the forests,	___	we won't go on holiday this year.
5	Will you help me later	___	if I gave you these comics?
6	If the farmers hadn't killed the buffalo,	1	the teacher wouldn't have been so angry.
7	Would you have eaten at an expensive restaurant	___	if I help you now?
8	If my dad doesn't find a job,	___	of course you won't do well.

Ⓒ Gebrauch

1 If Pat is at the party, **I'll (will) ask** her to dance with me.

2 We **would buy** a house if we **had** enough money.

3 If the Europeans **hadn't discovered** America, we **wouldn't have had** potatoes and coffee.

♦ Im *if*-Teil des Satzes drücken wir eine **Bedingung** aus; im Hauptteil stellen wir die **Folge** fest.

♦ Die drei Arten von *if*-Sätzen werden wie folgt gebraucht:

	if-Teil	Hauptteil	Zeitraum
fast sicher	*present*	*will ('ll)* + Grundform	Zukunft
höchst unwahrscheinlich	*simple past*	*would ('d)* + Grundform	Zukunft/ Gegenwart
völlig ausgeschlossen, da der Ausgang schon bekannt ist	*past perfect*	*would have*	Vergangenheit

❺ Vervollständige diese *if*-Sätze. Lies dir vorher den deutschen Satz gut durch, und entscheide, welchen Satztyp du jeweils benutzen mußt.

1 If the police had come (come) at once, they would have caught (catch) Freddy Fingers.

► Ich weiß schon, daß die Polizei Freddy Fingers nicht ertappt hat, also muß ich Typ [3] benutzen.

2 If Mr Bunn ____________ (give) her a job this summer, Alison ____________ (work) during the holidays.

► Alison wird bestimmt arbeiten, falls Mr Bunn ihr eine Stelle gibt, also muß ich Typ [ ] verwenden.

3 If the girls ________________ (not try) to climb the mountain last night, they ____________________________ (not get) lost.

▸ Ich weiß schon, daß die Mädchen sich gestern abend am Berghang verlaufen haben, also muß ich Typ ☐ benutzen.

4 Harry ________________ (have) less bad car accidents if he ________________ (not drive) so fast.

▸ Höchst wahrscheinlich wird Harry trotzdem weiterhin zu schnell fahren, also muß ich Typ ☐ benutzen.

5 Pat says she ________________ (go) back to live in Britain if she ________________ (find) a good job there.

▸ Vorausgesetzt, daß sie eine gute Stelle findet, wird Pat mit Sicherheit zurück nach Großbritannien gehen, also muß ich Typ ☐ benutzen.

6 Miss Pratt ________________ (do) interesting History projects with us if we ________________ (behave) better in lessons.

▸ Da die Klasse wahrscheinlich weiterhin den Geschichtsunterricht stören wird, muß ich Typ ☐ verwenden.

7 ____________________________ (you/buy) that T-shirt if it ________________ (be) still there?

▸ Da du bestimmt das T-Shirt kaufen wirst, falls es noch da ist, mußt du hier Typ ☐ benutzen.

6 Lies dir die Dialoge sorgfältig durch, und entscheide, um welchen Satztyp es sich handelt. Dann setze die Verben ein.

✔ = richtig; ✗ = falsch.

1 – It was lucky that the ambulance came so quickly yesterday.

✔ – Yes. If it had not come (not come) at once, old Mrs Cary ______________________ (die).

2 – Syd is horrible. He's so rude and bad-tempered. But he'll never change *(sich verändern)*.

– Yes, but if he ______________ (be) nicer, he ______________ ______________ (have) a much easier life.

3 – Come on, Jack. If we ______________________ (not leave) now, we ______________________ (be) late again.

– OK. Let's go.

4 – Mrs Green's parrot bit me today.

– Yes, but it was your fault. If you ______________________ (not put) your finger into his cage, he ______________ ______________ (not bite) you.

5 – If the settlers ______________________ (find) oil on the Sioux's land, the army ______________________ (put) them in a reservation, too.

– I know. That's what happened to a lot of tribes.

6 – Millions of Irish people went to live in the USA during the 19th century.

– Yes. If life in Ireland ______________________ (not be) so hard, they ______________________ (stay) at home.

– Oh, I don't know. If I ______________ (have) the chance, I ______________________ (like) to live in the USA.

– Yes, but that won't happen, will it?

max. 13

Weniger als 10 Punkte? Wenn ja, arbeite bitte die Aufgaben 4 und 5 nochmals durch!

Ein Säulenpuzzle

Jeder Satz läßt sich mit einem passenden Begriff aus dem Wortfeld *American Indians* vervollständigen. Wenn du die zehn richtigen Wörter in das Säulenpuzzle eingetragen hast, ergibt sich im stark umrandeten Feld eine Lösung.

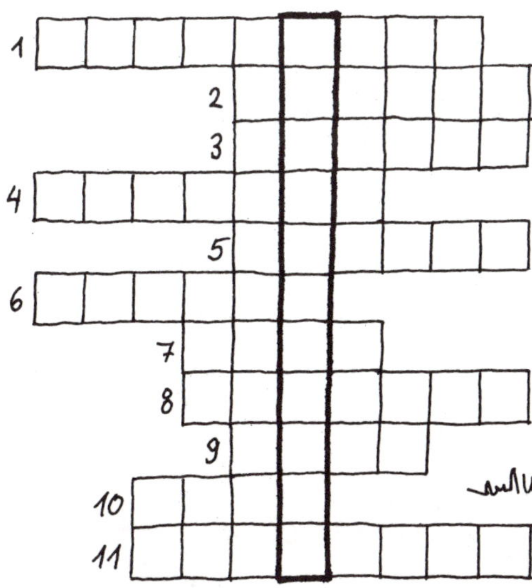

1 The Indians wore soft leather shoes called m...... .
2 The Indians hunted the ...... on the prairies for food and many other things they needed.
3 Geronimo was a famous chief of the A...... tribe.
4 The buffaloes gave the Indians ...... for shoes, clothes and tents.
5 The Apache and Sioux are famous Indian ....
6 The ...... is a kind of very light Indian tent.
7 Of course, the Indians killed the buffaloes to get ...... to eat, too.
8 The white settlers killed the buffaloes because they wanted the land for ....
9 The Indians made the buffalo ...... into leather and furs.
10 They made weapons, tools and jewellery *(Schmuck)* from the buffalo ....
11 Many white ...... did not understand the buffaloes were the Indians' "walking ▸ ______________________ ".

Suchwort

14

Die indirekte Rede (1)

A Die Zeitverschiebung
B Andere Änderungen

Wortfeld: Zusammenleben

Ⓐ Die Zeitverschiebung

1 *Mrs Todd* 'Oh Joe, you **are** late for lunch again.' Mrs Todd **told** Joe (that) he **was** late for lunch again.	simple present ▼ simple past
2 *Joe* 'Sorry, Mum. I **missed** the bus.' Joe said (that) he **had missed** the bus.	simple past ▼ past perfect
3 *Mr Todd* 'Again? You **are** always **missing** the bus.' Mr Todd said (that) Joe **was** always **missing** the bus.	present progressive ▼ past progressive
4 *Joe* 'I know, but I **was helping** Mrs Cary with her shopping.' Joe answered (that) he **had been helping** Mrs Cary with her shopping.	past progressive ▼ past perfect progressive
5 *Mr Todd* 'Fine, but you **have been** late home twice this week.' Mr Todd replied (that) Joe **had been** home late twice that week.	present perfect ▼ past perfect

6 *Joe* 'OK, I said I'm sorry. It **won't happen again.'** Joe promised (that) it **would not happen** again.	will-future ▼ would + infinitive
7 *Alison* 'You always say that. If I **had known** that you **had missed** the bus, I **wouldn't have hurried** myself.' Alison said (that) if she **had known** that Joe **had missed** the bus she **wouldn't have hurried** herself.	past perfect (1) would have + past participle (2) ▼ past perfect (1) would have + past participle (2)

♦ Wenn wir einem Dritten berichten wollen, was jemand anders gesagt hat, benutzen wir meistens die indirekte Rede. Es wird also nicht direkt zitiert, sondern berichtet.

♦ In der indirekten Rede benutzen wir ein *introductory verb* wie *tell, say, answer* usw., um zu zeigen, daß wir berichten.

♦ Wenn das *introductory verb* in der **Vergangenheit** steht, dann verschieben sich die Zeiten wie oben angezeigt.

1 Setze die folgenden direkten Äußerungen in die indirekte Rede. Benutze dabei jeweils das angegebene *introductory verb*.

1 *Mr Todd* 'I enjoyed the picnic very much.' (say)

Mr Todd said (that) he had enjoyed the picnic very much.

2 *Alison* 'Joe is an awful boy. He put a frog in my bed.' (shout)

Alison ________ (that) Joe ________ an awful boy because he ________ a frog in her bed.

3 *Mr Todd* 'Alison is just too serious. Of course Joe likes playing tricks on her.' (think)

Mr Todd ________ (that) Alison ________ ________ too serious, so of course Joe ________ playing tricks on her.

4 *Mrs Todd* 'Joe, I am pleased you help old Mrs Cary with her shopping so often.' (tell)

Mrs Todd ______________ (that) she ______________ pleased (that) he ______________ old Mrs Cary with her shopping so often.

5 *Joe* 'I'll wait for you outside the café Ben.' (promise)

Joe ______________ (that) he ______________ for Ben outside the café.

6 *Mrs Todd* 'Joe, Alison will be very angry with you if you play with her make-up again.' (say)

Mrs Todd ______________ (that) Alison ______________ ______________ very angry with Joe if he ______________ with her make-up again.

B Andere Änderungen

Joe 'Ben, I'll meet you here tomorrow, OK?'
Joe said **he** would meet **Ben/him at the café the next day.**

♦ In der indirekten Rede sind weitere Änderungen notwendig, wenn sonst die genauen Verhältnisse nicht unmißverständlich klar werden.

♦ Zeitadverbien müssen ebenfalls verändert werden, um die Zeitverhältnisse, d. h. die Zeitverschiebungen, zu verdeutlichen:

direkte Rede	indirekte Rede
now	► then
today	► that day
yesterday	► the day before
tomorrow	► the next/following day
the day after tomorrow	► two days later
the day before yesterday	► two days before
next week/year/...	► the following week/year/...
last week/year/...	► the previous week/year/...
a year ago	► a year before/earlier
this week	► that week

2 Setze Namen bzw. Pronomen ein, um den Sinn der direkten Äußerung genau wiederzugeben.

1 *Julie* 'I hope to see you and your brother at the party, Pam.'
Julie said she hoped to see ______ and ______ brother at the party.

2 *Joe* 'We are going on holiday with our best friends soon.'
Joe said ______ were going on holiday with ______ best friends soon.

3 *Mr Todd* 'I enjoyed our day in the country very much, Betty.'
Mr Todd said ______ had enjoyed ______ day in the country very much.

4 *Mrs Todd* 'Joe, you will miss your bus if you don't hurry up.'
Mrs Todd told him (that) he would miss his bus if he didn't hurry up.

5 *Gilda* 'I saw you in town. You were looking at some CDs, Hank.'
Gilda told her (that) she had seen her in town, and (that) she had been looking at some CDs.

3 Lies dir die Sätze durch und schreibe die Zeitadverbien auf, die du in der indirekten Rede benutzen würdest.

1 'I posted the card yesterday.' the day before
2 'I haven't seen him since last May.' the May before
3 'I start my new job next Monday.' the following Monday
4 'Jane lost £10 today.' that day
5 'Mr Bond can see you now.' then
6 'I got back the day before yesterday.' two days before
~~the day before today before~~
7 'I met Tim in June 1985.' in June 1985
8 'They're leaving this week.' that week

4 Lies dir den Dialog durch und setze dann die fehlenden Wörter und Ausdrücke in den Bericht ein. Beachte dabei die Änderungen, die bei der indirekten Rede notwendig sind.

✔ = richtig; ✗ = falsch.

Mrs Todd	Joe dear, I want you to come straight home from school today. We're visiting Aunt Mabel in hospital.
Joe	But I'm going to the cinema with Ben this afternoon. I can't come.
Alison	You're coming, Joe. You'll just have to go to the cinema tomorrow or something.
Joe	That'll be too late. The film changes tomorrow.
Mr Todd	Look, Joe, you were happy enough to see Aunt Mabel last Christmas when she gave you those lovely presents, weren't you? You had plenty of time then, didn't you? Well, now you can at least visit her when she is ill in hospital, OK?

✔ Mrs Todd told[1] Joe that ______[2] wanted ______[3] to come straight home from school because ______[4] to visit his Aunt Mabel in hospital. But Joe answered that he ______[5]. He ______[6] that ______[7] was going to the cinema with his friend Ben ______[8]. Alison ______[9] Joe that ______[10] was ______[11] to the hospital. She ______[12] that he ______[13] just ______[14] to the cinema ______[15]. Joe replied that that ______[16] too late as the film ______[17] the ______[18]. Then his father ______[19] that Joe ______[20] happy enough to see Aunt Mabel ______[21] when she ______[22] him a lot of presents. Mr Todd said that Joe ______[23] plenty of time then. Finally, Joe's father told him that he ______[24] at least visit ______[25] when ______[26] is ill in hospital.

max. 25

Weniger als 20 Punkte? Wenn ja, arbeite bitte die Aufgaben 1 bis 3 nochmals durch!

Schüttelwörter

Tim will unbedingt ein neues Fahrrad kaufen. Jedes Wochenende arbeitet er für seine Eltern, Verwandte und Nachbarn, um Geld zu verdienen.
Wenn du die Schüttelsätze unten richtig zusammenstellst, wirst du herausfinden, was Tim letztes Wochenende alles erledigt hat.

Tim ...

1 ... TWEN POGSHIPN ROF ISH NANRGY

went shopping

2 ... DEANLEC HET RAC ORF SIH RETHAF

3 ... TUDSED LAL TEH KOBOS

4 ... DAME EAT NO YUSDAN

5 ... KOOT DORUN A TOL FO REPAPS

6 ... DEKOOL REFTA HET YABB ON YADUSTAR

15

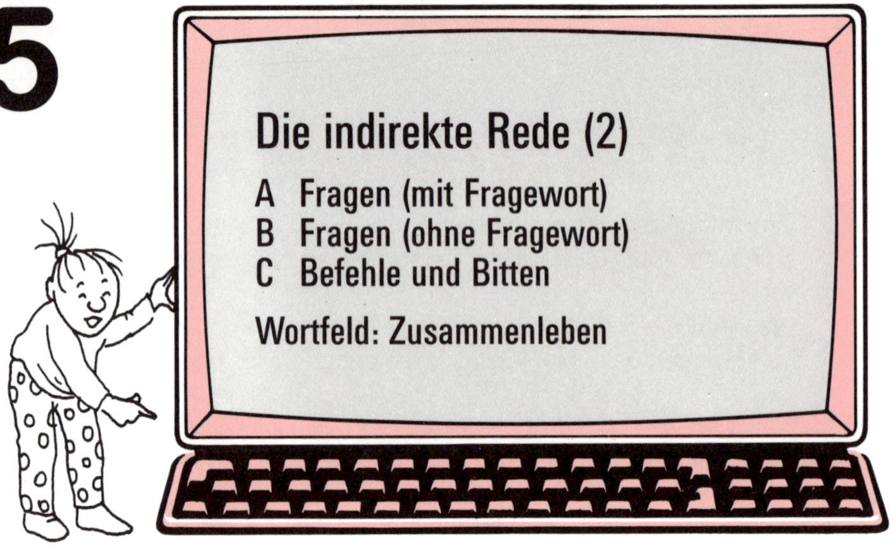

A Fragen (mit Fragewort)

1 *Julie* 'Where is my book?'
Julie **asked** where **her book was**.

2 *Ben* 'What are you doing tomorrow, Joe?'
Ben **asked Joe** what **he was doing the next day**.

3 *Alison* 'Who can we invite to our party?'
Alison **asked** who **they could invite** to **their** party.

4 *Mrs Todd* 'How much money have you got, Alison?'
Mrs Todd **asked Alison** how much money **she had got**.

♦ Wir leiten eine indirekte Frage mit *ask* ein.

♦ Indirekte Fragen haben die gleiche Satzstellung wie Aussagesätze, also Subjekt – Verb – Objekt.

♦ Das Fragezeichen (?) fällt natürlich weg.

♦ Änderungen, wie die Zeitverschiebung und die Umstellung der Zeitadverbien, die du aus indirekten Aussagesätzen kennst, müssen auch in indirekten Fragen vorgenommen werden.

1 Schreibe die Fragen unten in indirekte Fragen um.

Benutze durchweg *asked* als *reporting verb* und denke an alle Änderungen, die du durchführen mußt.

1 *Ann* 'Where did you park the car, Eve?'

Ann asked Eve here she had parked the car.

2 *Jim* 'How long have you had your car, Bill?'

Jim ______ Bill ______

______ car.

3 *Joe* 'How do you turn this CD-player on?'

Joe ______

CD-player on.

4 *Eve* 'What time will we see you tomorrow, Pat?'

Eve ______ Pat ______

______.

5 *Tim* 'Why didn't they come to Jim's party last week?'

Tim ______

to Jim's party ______.

6 *Pat* 'What can we do next weekend, Tim?'

Pat ______ Tim ______

______.

7 *Eve* 'When will you get home tonight, Jim?'

Eve ______

______.

8 *Ann* 'Where did you go for your holidays, Eve?'

Ann ______

______.

B Fragen (ohne Fragewort)

1 *Joe* 'Ben, can you come to my party on Saturday?'
Joe **asked** Ben **if/whether** he could come to his party the following Saturday.

2 *Mrs Todd* 'Joe, have you done your homework?'
Mrs Todd **asked** Joe **if/whether** he had done his homework.

♦ In Fragen **ohne Fragewort** benutzen wir *if* bzw. *whether*, um zu zeigen, daß es sich um eine Frage handelt. Alle sonstigen Änderungen sind dieselben wie bei Fragen mit Fragewort.

2 Schreibe die Fragen unten in indirekte Fragen um.
Benutze durchweg *if* bzw. *whether* und denke an alle Änderungen, die du durchführen mußt.

1 *Pat* 'Are they going to the dance tonight?'
Pat asked if (whether) they were going to the dance that night.

2 *Ann* 'Has she seen the new film at the ABC yet?'
Ann ______________________________
the new film at the ABC ______________________.

3 *Jim* 'Did you hear the weather forecast yesterday, Eve?'
Jim ____________ Eve ______________________
______________________________________.

4 *Tim* 'Do they like steaks?'
Tim ______________________________ steaks.

5 *Eve* 'Pat, can you get me some tea tomorrow?'
Eve ____________ Pat ______________________
some tea ______________________.

6 *Ben* 'Do we have to go to school next week?'
Ben ______________________________
to school ______________________.

3

Bei Carr's, einem Modegeschäft, ist eingebrochen worden. Inspector Harris stellt Mr Carr viele Fragen, die er für seinen Bericht braucht. Vervollständige den Bericht. Benutze dabei die indirekte Rede.

✔ = richtig; ✗ = falsch.

Harris	Mr Carr, when did you lock up the shop yesterday?
Carr	I left at about 9 p.m., Inspector.
Harris	Are you sure the shop was empty when you locked the door?
Carr	Yes, I am.
Harris	Can you tell me exactly what is missing, Mr Carr?
Carr	No, I can't tell you yet.
Harris	How did the thieves get into the shop?
Carr	Through a window.
Harris	Have you got an alarm, Mr Carr?
Carr	Yes, I have one, but only on the door.

✔ I asked[1] Mr J. Carr, the owner of the shop, ____________ ____________[2] up the shop ____________[3]. He said he had left at about 9 p.m. I then ____________[4] him ____________[5] that the shop ____________[6] empty when he ____________[7] the door, and Mr Carr replied that he was. When I ____________[8] him ____________[9] me exactly ____________ ____________[10], he said that he could not tell me yet. Then I asked ____________[11] into the shop, and Mr Carr answered that they had climbed in through a window. When I asked him ____________[12] an alarm, he replied that he had got one, but only on the door.

max. 11

Weniger als 8 Punkte? Wenn ja, arbeite bitte die Aufgaben 1 und 2 nochmals durch!

Ⓒ Befehle und Bitten

1 *Teacher* 'Stop talking and get on with your work, Joe.'
The teacher **told** Joe **to stop** talking and **to get on** with his work.

2 *Alison* 'Don't eat all the cake, please, Dad.'
Alison **asked** her father **not to eat** all the cake.

♦ Bei Befehlen benutzen wir *tell* und bei Bitten benutzen wir *ask* als *reporting verbs*.

♦ Das Vollverb erscheint als *to* + Infinitiv.

4 Mr und Mrs Todd fahren übers Wochenende weg. Sie sagen Alison und Joe, was sie während ihrer Abwesenheit alles machen sollen. Lies dir die beiden Listen durch und benutze die Buchstaben, um die direkten Befehle mit den entsprechenden indirekten Befehlen zu verbinden.

1 'Don't forget to water the plants.'

2 'Cut the grass, please, Joe.'

3 'Alison, remember to get some bread.'

4 'Joe, take out the rubbish, won't you?'

5 'Don't forget to switch off the TV.'

6 'Don't open the door to strangers.'

7 'Joe, help your sister, please.'

8 'Please don't quarrel, dears.'

A Mrs Todd asked Joe to help his sister.
B Mr Todd told Joe to cut the grass.
C Mrs Todd asked them not to quarrel.
D Mrs Todd told Alison not to forget to water the plants.
E Mrs Todd asked Alison to remember to get some bread.
F Mr Todd told Alison not to open the door to strangers.
G Mr Todd told Joe to take out the rubbish.
H Mr Todd asked both not to forget to switch off the TV.

1 D	2	3	4	5	6	7	8

5 Gib die Anweisungen der Polizeibeamten in der indirekten Rede wieder. Mit wem gesprochen wird, steht jeweils in Klammern am Satzende. Wenn *please* im Satz steht, benutze *asked*, sonst *told*.

1 *PC Davis* 'Move along, please.' (pedestrians)

PC Davis asked the pedestrians to move along.

2 *PC Smith* 'Don't touch anything.' (small boy)

PC Smith ______________________________

______________________________.

3 *PC Green* 'Let the ambulance through.' (some women)

PC Green ______________________________

______________________________.

4 *PC Smith* 'Go home.' (everyone)

PC Smith ______________________________.

5 *PC Green* 'Give me your name and address, please.' (Mrs Cary)

PC Green ______________________________

______________________________.

6 *PC Davis* 'Clean the blood off the road, please.' (a worker)

PC Davis ______________________________

______________________________.

7 *PC Smith* 'Don't smoke.' (a man)

PC Smith ______________________________.

6 In dieser gemischten Übung kommen Aussagesätze, Fragen (mit und ohne Fragewort) und Befehle vor.
Lies dir zunächst das Gespräch zwischen Alison, Joe und ihrer Mutter sorgfältig durch. Dann sage, was Mrs Todd am nächsten Tag ihrem Mann erzählt hat.

✔ = richtig; ✗ = falsch.

Mrs Todd	Oh, children. Stop quarrelling! What has gone wrong now?
Alison	Joe is a beast. He borrowed my new T-shirt yesterday, and look at it now. There's oil all over it. And I wanted to wear it tomorrow.
Joe	OK, OK. Don't keep shouting about it. I didn't do it on purpose *(absichtlich)*. It was an accident.
Mrs Todd	Oh, Joe. Why can't you be more careful, dear? I'm not surprised that Alison's upset.
Joe	All right, Mum. You're always on her side.
Mrs Todd	Now don't be rude, Joe. You know that's not true. But don't you think that Alison is right this time?
Joe	Well, I suppose she is right in a way.
Alison	He must buy me a new one, Mum.
Mrs Todd	Yes, Joe. I'm sorry, but you'll have to buy Alison a new T-shirt. Have you got enough money in your savings account *(Sparbuch)*?

– I'm afraid Alison and Joe had another quarrel yesterday, Jack.

– Oh dear. What did you do about it?

✔ – Well, first I told them to stop quarrelling and then I ____________________[1] wrong.
Alison told ____________________ ____________[2] new T-shirt ____________________[3], ...

– I think I know what's coming.

– Yes, Alison ____________________[4] at the T-shirt. There ____________________[5] oil all over it. And Alison ____________[6] that ____________________ ____________________[7].

– Well, she would say that, wouldn't she? And Joe?

– Anyhow, Joe ______________________________ [8] about it and ______________ [9] that ______________________ ____________ [10] it on purpose. He ______________________ ______________ [11] an accident.

– Of course. But he is very careless, isn't he?

– Yes, he is. I ____ [12] more careful, too. I ______________ [13] I ________________ ______________ [14] that Alison ______________ [15] upset.

– Oh dear. Joe didn't like that, did he?

– No, he didn't. He __________________________ [16] always on Alison's side.

– Oh, that's hard.

– Yes, it is. I ____________________________________ [17] rude, and that he ______________ [18] that ____________________ [19] true. Then I asked him if ______________________________ [20] that Alison ______________ [21] right ______________ [22] time, too.

– And?

– Well, Joe said he ____________________________________ [23] right in a way.

– Oh, I like that. Good old Joe.

– Yes, anyway, then Alison ______________________________ ______________ [24] a new T-shirt, and I ________________ ____________________________________ [25] a new one, too.

– I think you're right.

– Yes, I ____ [26] enough money in his savings account, and he said ...

max. 26

Weniger als 20 Punkte? Wenn ja, arbeite bitte die Aufgaben 4 und 5 nochmals durch!

Ein Quiz

Nur eine der angegebenen drei Möglichkeiten bildet einen sinnvollen Satz. Die Buchstaben hinter den richtigen Lösungen ergeben ein Motto für das Zusammenleben.

1 Ben, can you water the … please?
- car, (A)
- bathroom, (E)
- plants, (T)

2 Joe, stop … your sister.
- being polite to (O)
- teasing (A)
- helping (E)

3 A guide is someone who
- checks your train ticket. (M)
- helps you with your luggage. (L)
- shows you round old buildings. (K)

4 Colin likes food, so he wants to be a
- cook. (E).
- chemist. (I)
- waitress. (A)

5 Jim is a polite boy. He never
- helps his mother. (E)
- waits his turn. (U)
- forgets to say thank you. (I)

6 We are going to … on holiday.
- prison (P)
- the seaside (T)
- work (N)

7 At Christmas, nearly everyone
- goes to church. (R)
- goes to work. (Q)
- eats too much. (E)

8 I'm just going to buy some … for tea.
- fish (A)
- cigarettes (O)
- sweets (P)

9 The capital of Scotland is
- Glasgow. (J)
- Aberdeen. (R)
- Edinburgh. (S)

10 You're not allowed to
- take cats for walks. (B)
- smoke in the street. (P)
- cut the flowers in the park. (Y)

Das Motto ist: ______________________________.

16

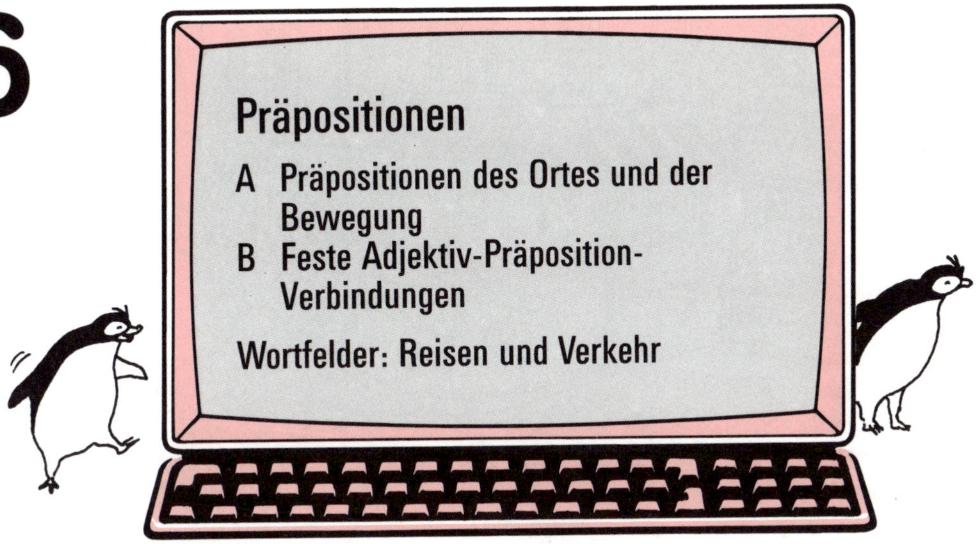

A Präpositionen des Ortes und der Bewegung

Erinnerst du dich?

[1] My grandad went **to** school **in** a small village **near** Wallingford **on** the Thames.

[2] An ambulance came **around** the corner and raced **down** the street.

- *To, in, near* usw. sind hier Präpositionen des Ortes [1].
- *Around* und *down* sind hier Präpositionen der Bewegung [2].
- Weitere Präpositionen kannst du dieser Tabelle entnehmen:

Ortspräpositionen

above/over	*über*	between	*zwischen*
(a)round	*rund/um*	in front of	*vor*
behind	*hinter*	in the middle of	*mitten (in/auf)*
below	*unter*	opposite	*gegenüber*

Präpositionen der Bewegung

across	*hinüber*	over	*über*
along	*entlang*	(a)round	*um/rundherum*
down	*hinunter*	through	*hindurch*
out of	*heraus*	to	*zu/nach/an*

1 Zunächst sieh dir die Straßenszene an. In den Texten hat der Schreibcomputer jeweils zwei Präpositionen eingesetzt, aber nur eine davon ist richtig. Lies dir die Texte sorgfältig durch und entscheide anhand des Bildes, welche der beiden unterstrichenen Präpositionen am besten paßt. Streiche dann die falsche bzw. wenig passende durch.

1 This is a street in/~~of~~ York. There is an ambulance racing along/across the street. The policeman in/on the middle from/of the road is stopping the cars so that the ambulance can get along/through the traffic into/to the hospital as quickly as possible.
2 The cars in front of/near and behind/next to the policeman are waiting for him to let them drive on.
3 Mr Chops the Butcher is coming from/out of his shop. He has got a bucket of water in/on his hand. He wants to throw the water on/over two dogs who are fighting in front of/near his shop.
4 At/near the traffic lights there is a boy with a skateboard on/under his arm. He wants to go across/through the street to/with his friend, who is waiting in/on the other side.
5 A bus is coming through/round the corner. It has a big 17 above/on top of the driver's window. It will stop at/near the bus-stop next to/outside Mr Bunn's shop. Mr Bunn is glad about the bus-stop right in front of/behind his shop. He often sells cakes to people waiting at/in the queue.

2 Manfred aus Nordhessen, Birgit aus Salzburg und Lars aus Hamburg haben alle Brieffreunde in England gefunden. Sie schreiben ihren Brieffreunden etwas über die Gegend, in der sie wohnen. Lies dir die Briefauszüge durch und setze die fehlenden Präpositionen ein.

✔ = richtig; ✗ = falsch.

1 My name is Manfred, and I live ________ Vöhl, a small village ________ the Edersee ________ the eastern part ________ Hesse ________ West Germany. Vöhl is ________ the small towns ________ Frankenberg and Korbach. You can drive ________ Kassel, which is the biggest town ________ our region in about an hour.

2 My name is Birgit. I come ________ Salzburg ________ the Austrian Tyrol. Mozart came ________ the city, and you can still go ________ the house where he was born. There are beautiful mountains and forests all ________ Salzburg, and tourists come here ________ all over the world to walk ________ the forests and to climb ________ the mountains.

3 My name is Lars Petersen, and I live ________ Hamburg, a big port ________ the Elbe ________ North Germany. We live ________ a part ________ Hamburg called Winterhude. The river Alster is ________ the end ________ our road. You can go ________ boat ________ the river and ________ a big lake which is also called the Alster. You can get out ________ the boat right ________ the middle ________ the city.

max. 30

Weniger als 25 Punkte? Wenn ja, arbeite bitte die Aufgabe 1 nochmals durch!

B Feste Adjektiv-Präposition-Verbindungen

1 – Alison is **afraid of** flying.
– I can understand that. I'm **worried about** all these plane crashes, too.

2 Julie is **good at** riding. She's very **interested in** horses.

3 Dad's **excited about** going through the Channel Tunnel.

♦ *Afraid of, worried about, good at, interested in* und *excited about* sind Beispiele fester Adjektiv-Präposition-Verbindungen.
Diese Zusammensetzungen mußt du immer als **ganze Vokabel** auswendig lernen.

♦ Die Verbindungen, die du bis jetzt kennengelernt hast, sind:

Präposition	Adjektiv-Verbindung
about	angry about, annoyed about, excited about, glad about, happy about, nervous about, pleased about (something), sorry about, worried about
at	bad at, good at
from	different from
in	interested in
of	afraid of, frightened of, tired of
with	bored with, pleased with (someone)

3 Hier sind einige Informationen über Molly und ihre Freunde. Vervollständige die Sätze auf Seite 117 anhand der Tabelle.

	good	bad	interested
Molly	Maths ***	History **	horses *
Ian	Sports ***	English ***	flying *
Jim	Sport **	Maths **	racing cars ***

*** = very good/bad/interested
** = quite good/bad/interested
* = good/bad/interested

1 Molly is very good at Maths, quite bad ________ History and is interested ________ horses.

2 Ian is very ________ Sport, very ________ English and is ________ ________ flying.

3 Jim is ________ Sport, quite ________ Maths and is ________.

4 Setze die Präpositionen ein.

✔ = richtig; ✗ = falsch.

– I'm really bored ________ [1] Martin.
– Oh? Why?
– Well, I said I'm good ________ [2] sport, so he immediately said that he's good ________ [3] sport, too.
– So what? What are you so annoyed ________ [4]? Martin's not bad ________ [5] sport, is he?
– Yes, but that's not what I mean. Look, I said I'm worried ________ [6] the German test, right? Then he says he's nervous ________ [7] it, too. I'm interested ________ [8] flying, and Martin? He's excited ________ [9] planes as well. I say I'm glad ________ [10] this and that. And what does Martin say? Go on, guess.
– Well, I suppose he says he's happy ________ [11] this and that, too.
– You're right. Why can't he be different ________ [12] me? I get so tired ________ [13] it.
– Well, that's the trouble with twin brothers, isn't it?

max. 13

Weniger als 10 Punkte? Wenn ja, arbeite bitte die Aufgabe 3 nochmals durch!

Wo sind die Präpositionen geblieben?

Vervollständige Alisons Brief an ihre deutsche Brieffreundin Jutta mit Präpositionen aus der Liste unten.

about – ago – at – before – for – from – in – near – of – on – outside – to – under – until

Dear Jutta!

My name is Alison Todd, and I'm 15. I got your letter ________ [1] my German teacher, Mr Wood, and I am very interested ________ [2] having a pen-friend ________ [3] Germany. I only started learning German ________ [4] September, so I'm not very good ________ [5] it yet. German is quite different ________ [6] English!

Now I want to tell you some details ________ [7] me and my family. We live ________ [8] the river at Thorpe, which is just ________ [9] Norwich. My dad is an engineer ________ [10] Norwich, and my mother has a part-time *(Teilzeit)* job ________ [11] the mornings, too. I have one brother, Joe. He is 12, and goes ________ [12] the same school as me. He is all right, but he likes playing tricks ________ [13] me. Sometimes I get very angry ________ [14] that. Two weeks

__________ 15 he put a dead mouse __________ 16 my pillow! What do you think __________ 17 that?

My favourite hobby is boating, but I am also interested __________ 18 history and nature. Please tell me __________ 19 your hobbies, too.

(But I'm very bad __________ 20 dancing, and I never go __________ 21 the disco!)

Mr Wood says you want to come __________ 22 England __________ 23 July. I am pleased __________ 24 that, because we will be __________ 25 home then. We are not going __________ 26 holiday __________ 27 August 8th.

Our school holidays start __________ 28 July 16th, so if you come __________ 29 then you can come __________ 30 school with me __________ 31 one or two days. Would you be interested __________ 32 doing that, or are you tired __________ 33 school?

Please write soon, I am already excited __________ 34 your visit.

Yours,

Alison